Jira 8 Administration Cookbook
Third Edition

Over 90 recipes to administer, customize, and extend Jira
Core and Jira Service Desk

Patrick Li

BIRMINGHAM - MUMBAI

Jira 8 Administration Cookbook
Third Edition

Copyright © 2019 Packt Publishing

Commissioning Editor: Richa Tripathi
Acquisition Editor: Chaitanya Nair
Content Development Editor: Rohit Kumar Singh
Senior Editor: Afshaan Khan
Technical Editor: Gaurav Gala
Copy Editor: Safis Editing
Project Coordinator: Vaidehi Sawant
Proofreader: Safis Editing
Indexer: Manju Arasan
Production Designer: Shraddha Falebhai

First published: July 2014
Second edition: May 2016
Third edition: June 2019

Production reference: 1250619

Published by Packt Publishing Ltd.
Livery Place
35 Livery Street
Birmingham
B3 2PB, UK.

ISBN 978-1-83855-812-3

www.packtpub.com

`Packt.com`

Subscribe to our online digital library for full access to over 7,000 books and videos, as well as industry leading tools to help you plan your personal development and advance your career. For more information, please visit our website.

Why subscribe?

- Spend less time learning and more time coding with practical eBooks and Videos from over 4,000 industry professionals

- Improve your learning with Skill Plans built especially for you

- Get a free eBook or video every month

- Fully searchable for easy access to vital information

- Copy and paste, print, and bookmark content

Did you know that Packt offers eBook versions of every book published, with PDF and ePub files available? You can upgrade to the eBook version at `www.packt.com` and as a print book customer, you are entitled to a discount on the eBook copy. Get in touch with us at `customercare@packtpub.com` for more details.

At `www.packt.com`, you can also read a collection of free technical articles, sign up for a range of free newsletters, and receive exclusive discounts and offers on Packt books and eBooks.

Contributors

About the author

Patrick Li is the cofounder of AppFusions and works there as a senior engineer. AppFusions is one of the leading Atlassian experts, specializing in integration solutions with many enterprise applications and platforms, including IBM Connections, Jive, Google Apps, and more. He has worked in the Atlassian ecosystem for over 9 years, developing products and solutions for the Atlassian platform and providing expert consulting services. He has authored many books and video courses covering Jira 4 to 8. He has extensive experience in designing and deploying Atlassian solutions from the ground up, and customizing existing deployments for clients across verticals such as healthcare, software engineering, financial services, and government agencies.

About the reviewers

Anutosh Ghosh has worked on Jira, Confluence, Trello, Bamboo, and few other Atlassian products, with a strong focus over the last 7 years on multiple Agile projects.

He believes in perfectionism and practical work wherever and whenever possible, which has been his USP throughout his 11.5 years of IT experience, spanning different technology-agnostic development and project management endeavors.

In today's technology-disruptive IT world, he still believes in constant learning and practicing different subject areas and skill sets (ranging from project management and soft skills, to framework architectures, and so on) to keep his mind refreshed and his knowledge up to date as much as possible.

Being a huge fan of Patrick Li, I'm honored to be able to review this book with the same zealous intent as when I read his previous Jira 6.x Administration Cookbook. Also, I wholeheartedly appreciate and thank both Heta and Vaidehi of the Packt team, whose relentless efforts and constant support helped me to complete the review of this book.

Last but not the least, I'm always indebted to God and my family for their motivation, support, and belief in me every time I'm feeling down.

Ripon Al Wasim is a software engineer living in Dhaka, Bangladesh. Ripon has 17 years' experience in the software industry.

He has a Level 3 Certification in the JLPT (Japanese Language Proficiency Test), and he has a bit of familiarity with Japanese culture, having worked in Japan as an IT professional.

Ripon is the author of the video course *Mastering Selenium Testing Tools*, by Packt Publishing, as has also reviewed other Packt titles, including *Selenium WebDriver Practical Guide*, *Performance Testing with JMeter – Second Edition*, *Mastering Selenium WebDriver*, and *Performance Testing with JMeter 3 – Third Edition*.

> *I would like to thank my mother and wife for creating a helpful and inspiring environment at home for me to study and review this book. I like to play and enjoy my free time with my twin babies, Nawar and Nazif.*

Packt is searching for authors like you

If you're interested in becoming an author for Packt, please visit authors.packtpub.com and apply today. We have worked with thousands of developers and tech professionals, just like you, to help them share their insight with the global tech community. You can make a general application, apply for a specific hot topic that we are recruiting an author for, or submit your own idea.

Table of Contents

Preface

Atlassian Jira is an enterprise-issue tracker system. One of its key strengths is its ability to adapt to the needs of the organization from the frontend user interface to provide a platform for third-party apps to extend its capabilities. However, understanding its flexibility and picking the right apps can often be a daunting task for many administrators. Learning how to take advantage of Jira's power while keeping the overall design simple and clean is important to the success of the implementation and future growth.

With this book, you can make full use of useful recipes with real-life Jira administration challenges, solutions, and examples. Each recipe contains easy-to-follow, step-by-step instructions and illustrations from the actual Jira application.

Who this book is for

This book is intended for administrators who customize, support, and maintain Jira for their organizations.

You will need to be familiar with, and have a good understanding of, Jira's core concepts. For some recipes, a basic understanding of HTML, CSS, JavaScript, and basic programming (Java or Groovy) will also be helpful.

What this book covers

Chapter 1, *Jira Server Administration*, contains recipes that help you administer your Jira server, including upgrading and securing Jira with the SSL certificate.

Chapter 2, *Customizing Jira for Your Projects*, contains recipes that allow you to customize Jira with custom fields and screens. This chapter also includes advanced techniques, such as using scripts and third-party apps to add more control to fields that are not available out of the box with Jira.

Chapter 3, *Jira Workflows*, covers one of the most powerful features in Jira, with recipes that show you how to work with workflows, including permissions and user input validation. This chapter also covers useful third-party apps and using scripts to extend out-of-the-box components.

Chapter 4, *User Management*, explains how users and groups are managed within Jira. It starts with simple recipes covering out-of-the-box user management features, and goes on to include topics such as LDAP integration and various single sign-on implementations.

Chapter 5, *Jira Security*, focuses on the different security control features offered by Jira, including different levels of permission and authorization control. This chapter also covers other security-related topics, such as user password policy and capturing electronic signatures.

Chapter 6, *Emails and Notifications*, explains Jira's email handling system for both outgoing and incoming emails. This chapter also covers Jira's event system and how to extend the basic set of events and templates.

Chapter 7, *Integrations with Jira*, covers how to integrate Jira with other systems, including other Atlassian applications and many other popular cloud platforms, such as Google Drive and GitHub.

Chapter 8, *Jira Troubleshooting and Administration*, covers the ways to troubleshoot various problems in Jira. Recipes include diagnosing common problems related to permissions and notification and more advanced features, where you, as the administrator, can mimic a user to better understand the problem.

Chapter 9, *Jira Service Desk*, covers Jira Service Desk, the new addition to the Jira platform. Jira Service Desk allows you to turn your Jira instance into a fully featured help desk system, leveraging Jira's powerful workflow and other customization features.

To get the most out of this book

For the installation and upgrade recipes, you will need to have the latest Jira 8 distribution, which you can download directly from Atlassian at the following link:

http://www.atlassian.com/software/jira/download

You may also require several additional pieces of software, including the following:

- Java SDK: You can get this from http://java.sun.com/javase/downloads.
- MySQL: You can get this from http://dev.mysql.com/downloads.

For other recipes, the details of where you can obtain the necessary tools are provided in the respective recipe.

Download the example code files

You can download the example code files for this book from your account at
www.packtpub.com. If you purchased this book elsewhere, you can visit
www.packtpub.com/support and register to have the files emailed directly to you.

You can download the code files by following these steps:

1. Log in or register at www.packtpub.com.
2. Select the **SUPPORT** tab.
3. Click on **Code Downloads & Errata**.
4. Enter the name of the book in the **Search** box and follow the onscreen instructions.

Once the file is downloaded, please make sure that you unzip or extract the folder using the latest version of:

- WinRAR/7-Zip for Windows
- Zipeg/iZip/UnRarX for Mac
- 7-Zip/PeaZip for Linux

The code bundle for the book is also hosted on GitHub at https://github.com/
PacktPublishing/Jira-8-Administration-Cookbook-Third-Edition. We also have other
code bundles from our rich catalog of books and videos available at https://github.com/
PacktPublishing/. Check them out!

Download the color images

We also provide a PDF file that has color images of the screenshots/diagrams used in this book. You can download it here:

https://static.packt-cdn.com/downloads/9781838558123_ColorImages.pdf.

Conventions used

There are a number of text conventions used throughout this book.

CodeInText: Indicates code words in text, database table names, folder names, filenames, file extensions, pathnames, dummy URLs, user input, and Twitter handles. Here is an example: "This is the template file for emails sent in HTML format, which is stored in the html subdirectory."

A block of code is set as follows:

```
#disable_html_escaping()

$eventTypeName - ($issue.key) $issue.summary
```

When we wish to draw your attention to a particular part of a code block, the relevant lines or items are set in bold:

```
<blockquote>
  <p>
   #if($comment.body)
      $comment.body
    #else
   <i>No comment</i>
```

Any command-line input or output is written as follows:

```
$ mkdir css
$ cd css
```

Bold: Indicates a new term, an important word, or words that you see on screen. For example, words in menus or dialog boxes appear in the text like this. Here is an example: "You can update this default scheme's notification settings by clicking on its **Notifications** link."

Warnings or important notes appear like this.

Tips and tricks appear like this.

Sections

In this book, you will find several headings that appear frequently (*Getting ready, How to do it..., How it works..., There's more...,* and *See also*).

To give clear instructions on how to complete a recipe, use these sections as follows:

Getting ready

This section tells you what to expect in the recipe and describes how to set up any software or any preliminary settings required for the recipe.

How to do it...

This section contains the steps required to follow the recipe.

How it works...

This section usually consists of a detailed explanation of what happened in the previous section.

There's more...

This section consists of additional information about the recipe in order to make you more knowledgeable about the recipe.

See also

This section provides helpful links to other useful information for the recipe.

Get in touch

Feedback from our readers is always welcome.

General feedback: Email `feedback@packtpub.com` and mention the book title in the subject of your message. If you have questions about any aspect of this book, please email us at `questions@packtpub.com`.

Errata: Although we have taken every care to ensure the accuracy of our content, mistakes do happen. If you have found a mistake in this book, we would be grateful if you would report this to us. Please visit `www.packtpub.com/submit-errata`, selecting your book, clicking on the Errata Submission Form link, and entering the details.

Piracy: If you come across any illegal copies of our works in any form on the internet, we would be grateful if you would provide us with the location address or website name. Please contact us at copyright@packtpub.com with a link to the material.

If you are interested in becoming an author: If there is a topic that you have expertise in, and you are interested in either writing or contributing to a book, please visit authors.packtpub.com.

Reviews

Please leave a review. Once you have read and used this book, why not leave a review on the site that you purchased it from? Potential readers can then see and use your unbiased opinion to make purchase decisions, we at Packt can understand what you think about our products, and our authors can see your feedback on their book. Thank you!

For more information about Packt, please visit packtpub.com.

Jira Server Administration 1

Atlassian Jira is a popular issue tracking system used by many companies across the Globe. One of its strengths, unlike most other enterprise software, is that it does not take days or weeks to install and implement, and is very simple to upgrade and maintain.

We will assume that you already know how to install a brand-new Jira system. So, we will explore common administration tasks, such as upgrading and migrating your Jira, and we'll look at different options, ranging from using the new automated upgrade utility provided by Atlassian to doing everything from scratch. We will also look at some other neat tricks for you as an administrator, such as resetting the admin password to get you out of sticky situations.

Since Jira is now a family of products, including Jira Core (which is the old Jira Classic before Jira 7), Jira Software (which is Jira Core plus agile capabilities), and Jira Service Desk (which is Jira Core plus the old Jira Service Desk add-on), recipes in this book will use the term Jira to refer to the most popular of the three, Jira Software.

In this chapter, we will cover the following topics:

- Installing Jira for production use
- Upgrading Jira with an installer
- Upgrading Jira manually
- Migrating Jira to another environment
- Setting up the context path for Jira
- Setting up SSL

- Installing SSL certificates from other applications
- Resetting the Jira administrator password
- Importing data from CSV
- Copying configurations between Jira instances

Installing Jira for production use

In this recipe, we will look at how to install and set up Jira in a production environment. This includes setting up a dedicated user to run Jira under and using an external database.

We will use the archive distribution since the steps are consistent across both the Windows and Linux platforms. This will also provide you with an insight into the exact steps required to get a Jira instance deployed and running; these would otherwise be hidden by an automated installer. This will provide you with the information needed for subsequent maintenance and further configurations.

Getting ready

The following things need to be checked before you begin with this recipe:

- Download the latest Jira archive distribution from https://www.atlassian.com/software/jira/download and select a package based on your server, such as Linux or Windows. For this recipe, we will be using the **TAR.GZ Archive**.
- Make sure your server environment meets Jira's requirements by visiting https://confluence.atlassian.com/adminjiraserver/supported-platforms-938846830.html.
- Install Java on the system. At the time of writing, Jira 8 requires Java 8 (either Oracle JDK or OpenJDK). You can download Java from https://www.oracle.com/technetwork/java/javase/downloads/index.html.
- Make sure that the JAVA_HOME or JRE_HOME environment variable is configured.
- Have a database system available, either on the server hosting Jira, or a different server accessible over the network. For this recipe, we will use **MySQL**. If you are using a different database, change the commands and queries accordingly.
- Download the necessary database driver. For MySQL, you can download it from https://dev.mysql.com/downloads/connector/j.

How to do it...

We first need to create an empty MySQL database for Jira:

1. Open up a new Command Prompt on the MySQL server.

2. Run the following command (you can also use another user instead of root as long as the user has permission to create new users and databases):

    ```
    mysql -u root -p
    ```

3. Enter the password for the user when prompted.

4. Create a new database for Jira by running the following command:

    ```
    create database jiradb character set utf8;
    ```

5. Create a new user for Jira in the database and grant the user access to the jiradb database we just created using the following command:

    ```
    grant all on jiradb.* to 'jirauser'@'localhost'
    identified by  'jirapassword';
    ```

6. In the previous five steps, we created a new database named jiradb and a new database user named jirauser. We will use these details later to connect Jira with MySQL. The next step is to install Jira.

7. Create a dedicated user account to run Jira under. If you're using Linux, run the following command as root or with sudo:

    ```
    useradd --create-home --comment "Dedicated
    Jira account" -- shell /bin/bash jira
    ```

> It is good practice to reduce security risks by locking down the user account so that it does not have login permissions.

8. Create a new directory on the filesystem where Jira will be installed. This directory will be referred to as JIRA_INSTALL.

9. Create another directory on the filesystem. This will be used for Jira to store its attachments, search indexes, application data, and other information. You can create this directory on a different drive with more hard disk capacity, such as a network drive (this could slow down performance). This directory will be referred to as JIRA_HOME.

It is good practice to keep the JIRA_INSTALL and JIRA_HOME directories separate; that is, the JIRA_HOME directory should not be a subdirectory inside JIRA_INSTALL. This will make future upgrading and maintenance easier.

10. Unzip the Jira archive file in the JIRA_INSTALL directory.

11. Change both the JIRA_INSTALL and JIRA_HOME directories' owner to the new Jira user.

12. Open the JIRA_INSTALL/atlassian-jira/WEB-INF/classes/jira-application.properties file in a text editor.

13. Locate the jira.home= line in this file.

14. Copy and paste this in the full path to the JIRA_HOME directory and remove the # symbol if present. Make sure you use the forward slash (/). The following line shows how it looks on a Linux system:

    jira.home=/opt/data/jira_home

Windows uses the backward slash (\) in the file path. You should still use the forward slash (/) while specifying the jira.home directory.

15. Copy the database driver JAR file (obtained from the *Getting ready* section) to the JIRA_INSTALL/lib directory.

16. Start up Jira by running the start-jira.sh (for Linux) or start-jira.bat (for Windows) script from the JIRA_INSTALL/bin directory as the Jira user. You should see the output, Tomcat, started in your console; this means that Jira is up and running.

17. Jira comes with a setup wizard that will help guide us through the final phase of the installation.
18. Open up a browser and go to `http://localhost:8080` (replace localhost with the actual server name). By default, Jira runs on port `8080`. You can change this by changing the connector port value in the `JIRA_INSTALL/conf/server.xml` file.
19. The first step in setup is to select how you want Jira to be set up. Select the **I'll set it up myself** option and click on the **Next** button:

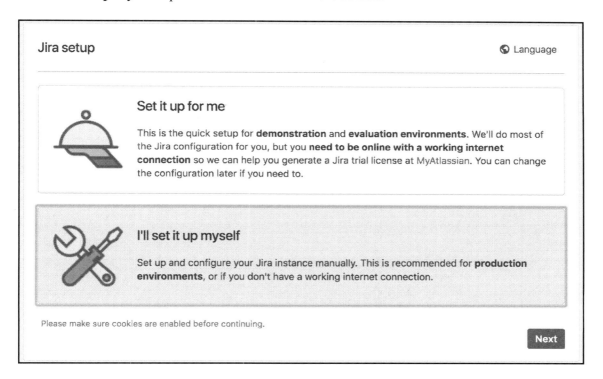

20. The second step is to set up database information. Select the **My Own Database (recommended for production environments)** option.
21. Select a value for the **Database Type** option. For this recipe, select the **MySQL 5.7+** option.

22. Enter the details for our new `jiradb` database:

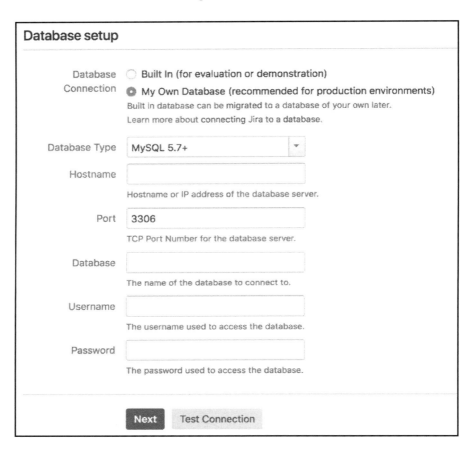

23. Click on **Test Connection** to check whether Jira is able to connect to the database.
24. Click on the **Next** button to proceed if the database connection test is successful and move to the next step of the wizard.
25. Enter the **Application Title** value for this Jira instance.
26. Select **Public** if you would like to let people sign up for accounts, or **Private** if you want only administrators to create accounts. Most organizations that use Jira to track internal projects will require **Private** mode.
27. Set the **Base URL** option. The base URL is the one that users will use to access Jira. Usually, this should be a fully qualified domain name or the hostname—that is, not localhost or an IP address.

28. Click on **Next** to go to the third step of the wizard, as shown in the following screenshot:

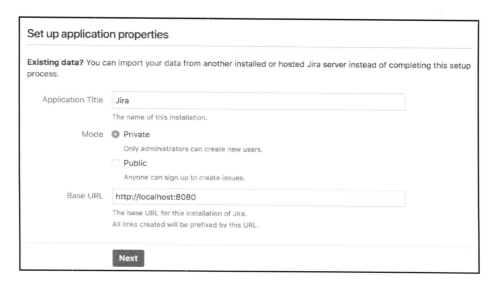

29. Enter your Jira license key if you have one. If you do not have a license key, you can generate a temporary trial license by clicking the **Generate a Jira trial license link** and following the instructions.

30. Click on **Next** to go to the fourth step in the wizard, as shown in the following screenshot:

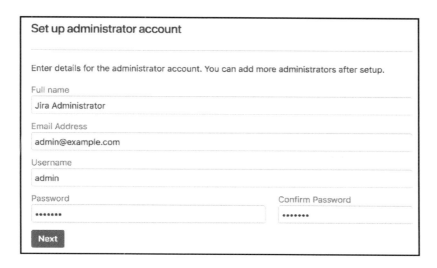

31. Enter the details for the initial administrator account. The user account will have access to all the configuration options in Jira, so make sure you do not lose its login credentials.

32. Click on **Next** to go to the fifth and final step of the wizard, as shown in the following screenshot:

33. Choose whether you want to set up an outgoing SMTP server **Now** or **Later**. If you do not have an SMTP server ready right now, you can always come back and configure it later.

34. Click on **Finish** to complete the setup process.

You will see the following **Welcome!** screen:

This ends the general configuration part of the setup process. Your Jira system is up and running. Next, Jira will walk you through its **onboarding** process as a first-time user. You will be asked to select the default language to use, upload a user avatar, and create your very first project.

There's more...

By default, Jira is set to use a maximum of 768 MB of memory. For a production deployment, you might need to increase the amount of memory allocated to Jira. You can increase this by opening up the `setenv.sh` (on Linux) or `setenv.bat` (on Windows) files in the `JIRA_INSTALL/bin` directory and changing the value of the `JVM_MAXIMUM_MEMORY` parameter.

For example, if we want to set the maximum memory to 2 GB, we will change it to `JVM_MAXIMUM_MEMORY="2048m"`. You will need to restart Jira after performing this change. For production uses, it is recommended that you allocate at least 4 GB (4096 MB) of memory to the Jira JVM. Make sure you have sufficient physical memory available on your server first.

If you are using LDAP for user management in your organization, refer to the *Integrating with LDAP for authentication only* recipe in `Chapter 4`, *User Management*.

Detailed steps for downloading the code bundle are mentioned in the *Preface* of this book. Please have a look. The code bundle for the book is also hosted on GitHub at `https://github.com/PacktPublishing/Jira-8-Administration-Cookbook-Third-Edition`. We also have other code bundles from our rich catalog of books and videos available at `https://github.com/PacktPublishing/`. Check them out!

Upgrading Jira with an installer

For both Windows and Linux, Atlassian provides an installer package that can guide you through the upgrade process. The installer will detect your current Jira installation and perform all the necessary tasks to upgrade it to the target version.

In this recipe, we will show you how to upgrade your Jira instance with the standard Jira installer.

Getting ready

As the Jira installer is only available for standalone installations on Windows and Linux, we will run you through the installer on Windows in this recipe:

- Check the upgrade notes for any special instructions as well as the target Jira version to make sure you can perform a direct upgrade.

- Make sure you have a valid Jira license.
- Verify whether your current host environment is compatible with the target Jira version. This includes the Java version, database, and OS.
- Verify whether your operating environment is compatible with the target's Jira version, specifically, the browser requirements.
- Make sure that the add-ons you are using are compatible with the new version of Jira.
- Download the installer binary for your target Jira version.

You can use the Universal Plugin Manager's Jira update check utility to check for add-on compatibility.

How to do it...

Upgrade your Jira system with the installer using the following steps:

1. Take your current Jira offline, for example, by running the `stop-jira.bat` script.
2. Back up the Jira database with its native backup utility.
3. Launch the installer and select the **Upgrade an existing JIRA installation** option.
4. Now, select the directory where the current Jira is installed:

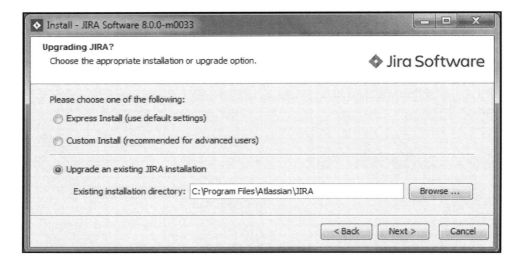

5. Check the backup JIRA home directory option and click on the **Next** button.

If your `JIRA_HOME` directory is big, you might want to manually back it up or remove some of the `cache` and `tmp` folders as it would take a long time for the installer to back these up.

6. Review the **Upgrade checklist** and click on the **Upgrade** button:

7. Wait for the installer to complete the upgrade process. Once the upgrade is complete, the installer will automatically launch Jira.
8. Update any add-ons once Jira starts successfully.

The installer will detect and provide you with a list of customized files in the `JIRA_INSTALL` directory, which you will need to copy manually after the upgrade.

See also

If you cannot use the installer to upgrade Jira, refer to the *Upgrading Jira manually* recipe.

Upgrading Jira manually

If you find yourself in a situation where you cannot use the installer to upgrade Jira—for example, if you are hosting Jira on an OS that does not have an installer binary or on a cloud platform, then you can use the manual upgrade method to upgrade your Jira instance.

Getting ready

The tasks required to upgrade Jira manually will remain the same as those for the installer. Refer to the previous recipe for common tasks involved. As the installer automates many backup tasks while upgrading Jira manually, you will have to do the following:

1. Back up the Jira database with its native backup utility.
2. Back up the `JIRA_INSTALL` directory.
3. Back up the `JIRA_HOME` directory.
4. Get a list of all the customized files in the `JIRA_INSTALL` directory from the **System Info** page in Jira.

How to do it...

To manually upgrade your Jira instance, perform the following steps:

1. Take your current Jira offline.
2. Install the new version of Jira in a different directory.
3. Edit the `jira-application.properties` file in the `JIRA_INSTALL/atlassian-jira/WEB-INF/classes` directory to point to the existing `JIRA_HOME` directory.
4. Copy any modified files from the old Jira instance to the new one.
5. Start up the new Jira instance.
6. Update the add-ons once Jira starts successfully.
7. Remove the previous installation directory to avoid confusion.

How it works...

What we did here essentially involved setting up a new instance of Jira and pointing it at the old Jira instance's data. When we start up the new Jira instance, it will connect to the existing Jira database by reading the dbconfig.xml file from the JIRA_HOME directory, and will perform an in-place upgrade to make all the necessary schema changes.

Migrating Jira to another environment

Now that we have gone through upgrading a Jira instance, we will look at how to move a Jira instance to another server environment. This is a common use case when you need to move an application to a virtualized environment or data center.

Getting ready

The following things need to be checked before you start with this recipe:

- Make sure you have a valid Jira license.
- Check whether your new environment is compatible with Jira system requirements.
- Ensure that both the old and new Jira instances are of the same major or minor version. If you intend to run a newer version of Jira in the new environment, it is recommended that you upgrade once the migration is successful.

 Migrating a system can be very disruptive for users. Make sure you communicate this to your users and allocate sufficient time for rollbacks.

How to do it...

To migrate an existing Jira instance to another server, perform the following steps:

1. Download and install a brand-new Jira instance in your new environment with an empty database.

2. Note down the files listed under **Modified Files** and **Removed Files** in the **System Info** page for your current Jira. The following screenshot shows an example:

Modified Files	[Installation Type: Standalone] jira-application.properties, WEB-INF/web.xml
Removed Files	[Installation Type: Standalone] There have been no removed files

3. Shut down your current Jira instance.
4. Back up your current Jira database with the database's native backup utility.
5. Back up your current JIRA_HOME directory.
6. Take your new Jira offline.
7. Copy over your JIRA_HOME backup and replace the new JIRA_HOME directory with it.
8. Update the dbconfig.xml file with the new Jira database details.
9. Copy your database backup and restore the new Jira database.
10. Start up the new Jira instance.
11. Apply the same changes to the new Jira instance from step 2.

Setting up the context path for Jira

If you have multiple web applications running on the same domain, you might want to set up a context path for Jira—for example, http://example.com/jira, where /jira is the context path.

How to do it...

Perform the following steps to set up a context path for Jira:

1. Shut down Jira if it is running.
2. Open up JIRA_INSTALL/conf/server.xml in a text editor.

3. Locate the following line and enter the context path for the `path` attribute—for example, `path="/jira"`:

```
<Context path="/jira"docBase="${catalina.home}
/atlassian-jira" reloadable="false"
useHttpOnly="true">
```

4. Save the file and restart Jira. If you are doing this after Jira has been installed, you will have to update Jira's base URL option so that its links will reflect the change.
5. Log into Jira as an administrator.
6. Navigate to **Administration > Systems > General Configuration**.
7. Click on the **Edit Settings** button.
8. Enter the fully qualified URL in Jira, including the context path, in the **Base URL** field.
9. Click on **Update** to apply the change.

After you have all this set up, you will be able to access Jira with the new context path, and all the links, including those from Jira's notification emails, will be the context path in the URL.

Setting up SSL

By default, Jira runs with a standard non-encrypted HTTP protocol. This is acceptable if you are running Jira in a secure environment, such as an internal network. However, if you plan to open up access to Jira over the internet, you need to tighten up security by encrypting sensitive data, such as the usernames and passwords that are sent, by enabling HTTP over **SSL (HTTPS)**.

This recipe describes how to install SSL on the Jira Tomcat application server. If you have an HTTP web server such as Apache in front of Jira, you can install the SSL certificate on the web server instead.

Getting ready

You need to have the following set up before you can step through this recipe:

1. **Obtain a valid SSL certificate**: You can either use a self-signed certificate or obtain one from a **certificate authority (CA)** such as **Verisign**. Using a self-signed certificate will display a warning message when users first visit the site, as shown in the following screenshot:

The site's security certificate is not trusted!

You attempted to reach **localhost**, but the server presented a certificate issued by an entity that is not trusted by your computer's operating system. This may mean that the server has generated its own security credentials, which Chrome cannot rely on for identity information, or an attacker may be trying to intercept your communications.

You should not proceed, **especially** if you have never seen this warning before for this site.

(Proceed anyway) (Back to safety)

▶Help me understand

2. Ensure that the JAVA_HOME environment variable is set properly.
3. Make sure you know which JDK/JRE Jira is using. You can find this information from the **System Info** page in Jira, where you need to look for the java.home property.
4. Make sure your JRE/JDK's bin directory is added to your PATH environment variable, and the keytool command will output its usage, as shown in the following screenshot:

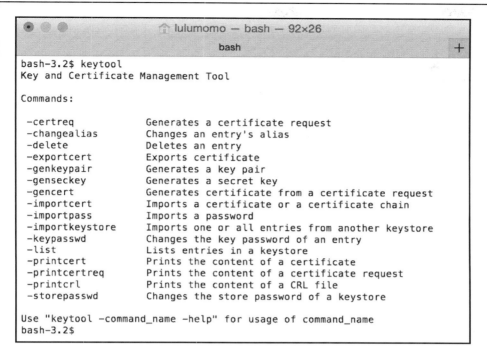

```
bash-3.2$ keytool
Key and Certificate Management Tool

Commands:

 -certreq          Generates a certificate request
 -changealias      Changes an entry's alias
 -delete           Deletes an entry
 -exportcert       Exports certificate
 -genkeypair       Generates a key pair
 -genseckey        Generates a secret key
 -gencert          Generates certificate from a certificate request
 -importcert       Imports a certificate or a certificate chain
 -importpass       Imports a password
 -importkeystore   Imports one or all entries from another keystore
 -keypasswd        Changes the key password of an entry
 -list             Lists entries in a keystore
 -printcert        Prints the content of a certificate
 -printcertreq     Prints the content of a certificate request
 -printcrl         Prints the content of a CRL file
 -storepasswd      Changes the store password of a keystore

Use "keytool -command_name -help" for usage of command_name
bash-3.2$
```

Now let's get started with the steps for this recipe.

How to do it...

Perform the following steps to import an SSL certificate:

1. Open up a command window and go to the directory where the certificate file resides.
2. Generate a **Java KeyStore (JKS)** for Jira by running the `keytool -genkey -alias jira -keyalg RSA -keystore $JIRA_HOME/jira.jks` command.
3. Import the certificate into the KeyStore repository by running the `keytool -import -alias jira -keystore $JIRA_HOME/jira.jks -file file.crt` command, where `file.crt` is the certificate file.
4. Open the `server.xml` file located in the `JIRA_INSTALL/conf` directory in a text editor.

5. Locate and uncomment the following XML configuration snippet:

```
<Connector port="8443"
maxHttpHeaderSize="8192" SSLEnabled="true"
maxThreads="150"
minSpareThreads="25" maxSpareThreads="75"
enableLookups="false"
disableUploadTimeout="true"
acceptCount="100" scheme="https" secure="true"
clientAuth="false"
sslProtocol="TLS" useBodyEncodingForURI="true"/>
```

6. Add a few new attributes to the `Connector` tag and save the file, as follows:

```
keystoreFile="PATH_TO_YOUR_KEYSTORE"
keystorePass="PASSWORD_FOR_YOUR_KEYSTORE"
keyAlias="jira"
keystoreType="JKS"
```

7. Restart Jira to apply the changes.

How it works...

We first created a new Java KeyStore repository for Jira to store its own SSL certificate with Java's keytool utility. During this step, you are prompted to provide information about the store as well as a password to access the KeyStore repository.

 Do not lose the password to the KeyStore repository.

After we created the KeyStore repository, we imported the certificate (and then enabled an additional connector to listen for HTTPS connections) by uncommenting the connector XML tag. We also added new attributes to the tag so that Tomcat knows where our new KeyStore repository is and how to access it to get to the certificate.

You can also change the port number for the connector if you want to run HTTPS on a more common port, 443, instead of the default port, 8443, and your final XML snippet will look something similar to the following:

```
<Connector port="443"
maxHttpHeaderSize="8192" SSLEnabled="true" maxThreads="150"
minSpareThreads="25"
maxSpareThreads="75" enableLookups="false"
disableUploadTimeout="true" acceptCount="100"
scheme="https" secure="true" clientAuth="false"
sslProtocol="TLS" useBodyEncodingForURI="true"
keystoreFile="/opt/jira/jira.jks"
keystorePass="changeme"
keyAlias="jira" keystoreType="JKS"/>
```

There's more...

At this point, users can access Jira with both HTTP and HTTPS, and you need to configure Jira so that it will automatically redirect all HTTP traffic to HTTPS. Jira comes with a handy configuration utility that can help you set up this configuration.

 You should first make sure your HTTPS configuration is working correctly before attempting this recipe.

Perform the following steps:

1. Open the Command Prompt and go to the `JIRA_INSTALL/bin` directory.
2. Depending on your OS, run the `config.bat` (Windows) or `config.sh` (Linux / OS X) file.
3. Select the **Web Server** tab from the **JIRA Configuration Tool** window.
4. Select the **HTTP and HTTPs (redirect HTTP to HTTPs)** option for **Profile**.
5. Click on the **Save** button at the bottom of the window, as shown in the following screenshot.

6. Restart Jira to apply the change:

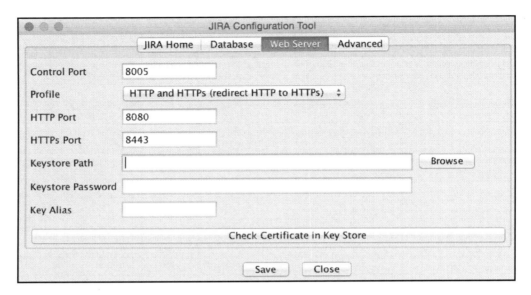

If you cannot use the **JIRA Configuration Tool**, you can perform the following steps to set up the configuration manually:

1. Open the `web.xml` file located in the `JIRA_INSTALL/atlassian-jira/WEB-INF` directory.

2. Add the following XML snippet at the end of the file just before the closing `</webapp>` tag:

```
<security-constraint>
 <display-name>HTTP to HTTPs Redirection</display-name>
<web-resource-collection>
 <web-resource-name>all-except-
 attachments</web-resource-name>
 <url-pattern>*.jsp</url-pattern>
 <url-pattern>*.jspa</url-pattern>
 <url-pattern>/browse/*</url-pattern>
</web-resource-collection>
<user-data-constraint>
 <transport-guarantee>CONFIDENTIAL</transport-guarantee>
 </user-data-constraint>
</security-constraint>
```

3. Restart Jira to apply the change.

See also

For information on connecting Jira to other applications that run on SSL, refer to the next recipe.

Installing SSL certificates from other applications

You might need to connect Jira to other services, such as LDAP, mail servers, and other websites. Often, these services make use of SSL. In such cases, the connection will fail, and you will see the following errors in your Jira log file:

```
javax.net.ssl.SSLHandshakeException:
sun.security.validator.ValidatorException: PKIX path building failed:
sun.security.provider.certpath.SunCertPathBuilderException: unable to find
valid certification
path to requested target
```

Getting ready

For this recipe, we will use the Java keytool utility, so make sure you have the following configuration set up:

- Obtain the required SSL certificate from the target system.
- Ensure that the JAVA_HOME environment variable is set properly.
- Make sure you know which JDK/JRE Jira is using. You can find this information on the **System Info** page, where you need to look for the java.home property.
- Make sure your JRE/JDK's bin directory is added to your PATH environment variable, and the keytool command will output its usage.
- Obtain the password for the Java trust store used by Jira.

How to do it...

In this recipe, let's assume we want to connect Jira to an LDAP server that is running on SSL. Perform the following steps to make it a trusted site inside Jira:

1. Open up a Command Prompt and go to the directory where the certificate file resides.

2. Import the certificate into the trust store by running `keytool -import -alias tomcat -file file.cer $JAVA_HOME/jre/lib/security/cacerts` command, where `file.cer` is the certificate file.

3. Restart Jira to apply the changes.

How it works...

When Jira attempts to connect to an SSL-protected service, it will first check whether the target service's certificate can be trusted. This is done by checking to see whether the certificate is present in what is called the Java trust store. If the certificate is not present, the connection will fail.

The trust store is a special KeyStore repository, usually called `cacerts`, and is located in the `$JAVA_HOME/lib/security` directory on the server.

We used the keytool utility to import the certificate to our local trust store, so the target service will be registered as a trusted service and will allow Jira to connect to it successfully.

Resetting the Jira administrator password

Sometimes, you might forget or lose the password to the account with the Jira administrator or Jira System Administrator permission, and you cannot retrieve it using the password reset option. For example, suppose Jira does not have an SMTP server configured, or you restored Jira from a data dump and do not know the account and/or password. In these cases, you need to reset the administrator password directly in the database.

 This recipe only applies to Jira instances that use the default internal user directory option. External user management, such as LDAP, will not work with this recipe.

Getting ready

As we will reset the password stored in Jira's database, make sure you do the following:

- Connect to the Jira database via either the command line or a GUI.
- Update the Jira database records.

How to do it...

Let's assume we use the default `mysql` command-line tool and MySQL as the backend database for Jira. If you are using a different database, you may need to change the following SQL statements accordingly:

1. Connect to the Jira database with a client tool by running the `mysql -u jirauser -p` command, where `jirauser` is the username used by Jira to access the Jira database.

2. You can find Jira's database details from the `dbconfig.xml` file located in `JIRA_HOME`.

3. Change to the Jira database by running the `use jiradb` command, where `jiradb` is the name of Jira's database.

4. Determine the groups that have the Jira System Administrator global permission with the following SQL statement:

   ```
   select perm_parameter from
   schemepermissions where PERMISSION=44;
   ```

5. Find users that belong to the groups returned in the previous step by running the following SQL statement, where `jira-administrators` is a group returned from the previous step:

   ```
   select child_name, directory_id
   from cwd_membership where
   parent_name='jira-administrators';
   ```

The `jira-administrators` group is the default group that administrators belong to. You might get a different group if you customize the permission configurations. The table column for the username is `child-name`.

6. Reset the user's password in the database with the following SQL statement, where `admin` is a user returned in the previous step:

```
update cwd_user set
credential='uQieO/1CGMUIXXftw3ynrsaYLShI+
GTcPS4LdUGWbIusFvHPfUzD7
CZvms6yMMvA8I7FViHVEqr6Mj4pCLKAFQ==' where
user_name='admin';
```

7. Restart Jira to apply the change.

How it works...

With Jira's internal user directory, all user and group data is stored in the Jira database. The value `44` is the ID of the Jira System Administrator global permission.

If you do not know which groups or users are granted the Jira System Administrator global permission, you will first have to find this information using steps 4 and 5. Otherwise, you can skip to step 6 in order to reset the password.

Jira's user password is stored in the `cwd_user` table. As Jira only stores the hash value of the password, we changed the user's admin password hash to `uQieO/1CGMUIXXftw3ynrsaYLShI+GTcPS4LdUGWbIusFvHPfUzD7CZvms6yMMvA8I7FV iHVEqr6Mj4pCLKAFQ==`, which is the **UTF-8**-encoded hash value of `sphere`.

Importing data from CSV

Often, you will need to import data from other systems into Jira. For example, you might want to migrate data from an older bug-tracking system, or if you have data coming out of other systems, you may want to use this output to populate your project.

As systems often have their own data structure, it is often not this straightforward to perform data migration. However, the good news is that most systems can export data in CSV (or Excel, which can be easily transformed into CSV format); we will look at using CSV as a way to import data into Jira in this recipe.

Getting ready

When importing data into Jira, the most important thing is to prepare your input data file and make sure it is formatted correctly and contains all the necessary information. To help the importer, keep the following in mind:

- Remove any non-data-related content, especially if you created your CSV file from a spreadsheet, which will help to keep the file size down.
- If your file contains users who need to be imported into fields such as **Assignee**, make sure you use either their usernames or email addresses that can be matched against corresponding accounts in Jira.
- If your file contains dates that need to be imported into fields, such as `Due date`, make sure they are all formatted using the same date format. This is so that Jira can process date values consistently.

How to do it...

To import data from other systems, perform the following steps:

1. Log in to Jira as an administrator.
2. Select the **Projects** menu from the top and select the **Import External Project** option.
3. Select the **CSV** option. If, however, you see your system in the list, you can choose that instead. The process of using a system-specific importer will be mostly the same as the CSV importer, with some minor differences.

4. Select the CSV file for the **CSV Source File** field. If you are performing an import for the first time, do not select the **Use an existing configuration** option. We will generate the configuration at the end of the import, and you will be able to use this to fast-track future imports.

5. Expand the **Advanced** option if your file uses a different file encoding or uses a character other than a comma (,) as its separators. Click on the **Next** button to proceed to step 2 of the wizard:

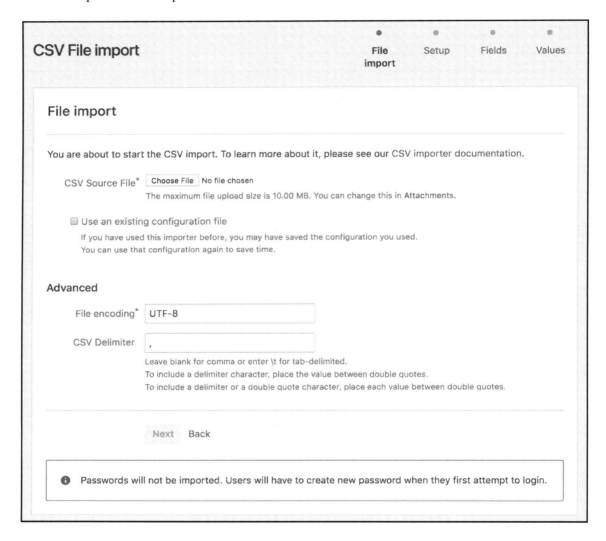

6. Select the project to import your data into. If you do not have a project, you can select the **Select New** option and create a project on-the-fly.

Generally, it is best to have the project created beforehand to ensure that it is set up with the correct configuration schemes, such as the workflow and fields.

7. Verify the **E-mail Suffix for New Users** and **Date format** values used in your CSV file. This will ensure that data such as dates will be correctly parsed while being imported and saved in Jira's date fields, such as `Due dates`:

8. Select and map the CSV columns to Jira fields. Certain fields, such as the **Summary** field, must have a corresponding column in the file; otherwise, Jira will not allow you to proceed. If you do not want to map a column, you can select the **Don't map this field** option.

9. Select the **Map field value** option for any columns mapping to a selected list style field. This will allow you to map individual values from the CSV file column to options available in Jira. Unless you are sure that your file contents can be mapped to the Jira field options exactly, it is best to manually verify this; otherwise, you will end up with duplicated values due to, for example, case sensitivity:

10. If you opt to map field values, review all of the listed values and map them to their corresponding field options in Jira. If a value does not have an option, you can type in the desired option and Jira will create it.

11. Click on the **Begin Import** button to start importing your data into Jira:

12. After the import process is completed, review the result. You can click on the **Download a detailed log** link to get a full log of the process if the import fails. You can also click on the **Save the configuration** link to get a copy of the mapping files so that, next time, you do not have to remap everything from scratch.

There's more...

Using CSV files to import custom data into Jira is the most versatile approach since many systems can export their data into CSV. However, as you will have noted already, Jira comes with a number of specialized importers for various systems. These importers often have additional features to help with data import. The Atlassian Marketplace website (`https://marketplace.atlassian.com`) also has a number of importers created by third parties. If you do not see your system listed in the out-of-the-box importers, make sure you do a search in the marketplace and check whether someone has already created an importer for it.

Copying configuration settings between Jira instances

If you have a controlled IT environment where changes need to go through development, testing/staging, and production processes, then, without a doubt, you will know how painful it is to promote Jira configuration changes across different environments. Since Jira does not provide a way to export configurations out of the box, all changes will need to be manually applied to each environment, which is both time-consuming and error-prone.

In this recipe, we will look at using a specialized tool that can help to make this process easier.

Getting ready

For this recipe, we need to have the Configuration Manager for Jira add-on installed on both the source Jira instance as well as the target Jira instance. You can install it directly from the Universal Plugin Manager, or download it from the following link: `https://marketplace.atlassian.com/plugins/com.botronsoft.jira.configurationmanager`.

How to do it...

The Configuration Manager for Jira add-on requires you to first create a snapshot. A snapshot contains all the configuration settings you want to copy over to a different Jira instance.

You can create two types of snapshot:

- **System**: This includes all configurations in Jira.
- **Project**: This includes only configurations required for the selected project.

Proceed with the following steps to create a configuration snapshot:

1. Navigate to **Administration** > **Configuration Management** > **Snapshots**.
2. Click on the **Add Snapshot** button.
3. Opt to create either a **System Configuration** or **Project Configuration** snapshot.
4. Enter a name for the snapshot.
5. Click on the **Create** button. The following screenshot shows the details of the snapshot we created:

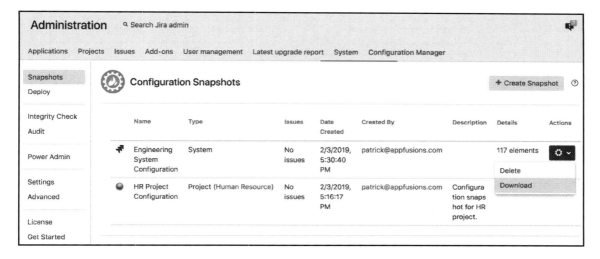

Having created the snapshot, there are several ways in which we can promote and deploy changes to another Jira instance. We can either download the snapshot ZIP file and upload it or link the two Jira instances together with Application Link and load the snapshot remotely. We will use the snapshot file option in this recipe. Proceed with the following steps to deploy a snapshot:

1. Log in to the other Jira instance as an administrator.
2. Navigate to **Administration** > **Configuration Management** > **Deploy.**
3. Select the **From Snapshot File** option.
4. Choose the snapshot ZIP file.
5. Click on the **Deploy** link to start the deployment.

The add-on will walk you through a deployment wizard, where it will analyze the contents of the snapshot and determine whether your current Jira system meets all the necessary requirements. For example, in the following screenshot, it has informed us that there is an add-on version mismatch:

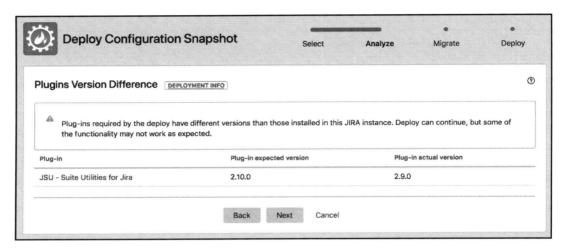

After the add-on has determined that all the requirements are met, it will provide a quick summary of all the changes that will be applied (seen in the following screenshot). This is a good time to review the list of items to make sure we are not introducing unwanted changes accidentally, as shown in the following screenshot:

If everything looks good, we can finish migrating the configuration changes and deploy them to the target instance.

2
Customizing Jira for Your Projects

An information system such as Atlassian Jira is only as useful as the data that goes into it, so it is no surprise that Jira is very flexible when it comes to letting you customize the fields and screens. Jira comes with a suite of default fields to help you get it up and running quickly, and it also allows you to add your own fields, called custom fields, to address your unique needs.

In this chapter, we will learn not only how to manage these custom fields in Jira, but also how you can create your very own custom field types with your own business logic, through scripting.

In this chapter, we will cover the following topics:

- Setting up different issue types for projects
- Making a field required
- Making the assignee field required
- Hiding a field from view
- Creating a new field configuration
- Setting up customized screens for your project
- Removing a select list's **None** option
- Adding help tips to custom fields
- Using JavaScript with custom fields
- Setting default values for fields
- Adding permission to fields
- Creating your own custom field types

Setting up different issue types for projects

Jira comes with a number of issue types out of the box that are designed for software project management. However, over time, you might find that these issue types do not apply to all of your projects, and you have added your own. In this recipe, we will look at how to manage the issue types, so that each project can have its own set of issue types.

How to do it...

Proceed with the following steps to set up a project-specific issue type list:

1. Log into Jira with a user that has a Jira administrator's permission.
2. Navigate to **Administration** > **Issues** > **Issue type schemes**.
3. Click on the **Add issue type scheme** button.
4. Enter the name for the new issue type scheme.
5. Add issue types to the scheme by dragging them from right to left.
6. Select the default issue type.
7. Click on the **Save** button to create the new scheme, as shown in the following screenshot:

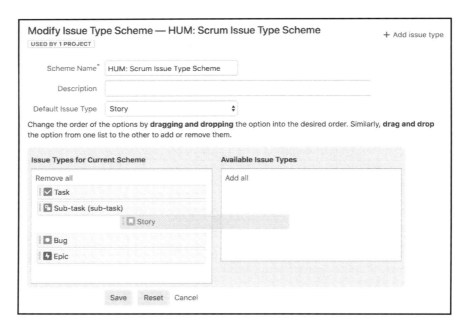

Having created your new issue type scheme, you now need to apply it to projects in which you want to restrict issue type selections:

1. Click on the **Associate** link for the new issue type scheme.
2. Select the project(s) you want to apply the scheme to.
3. Click on **Associate** to change the selected projects' issue type scheme.

If the project has issues with issue types that do not exist in the new issue type scheme, Jira will walk you through a migration process where you can update the issue type for all the impacted issues.

Making a field required

Required fields such as **Summary** and **Issue Type** have a little red asterisk next to them, which means they must have a value when you are creating or updating an issue. This is a great way to ensure that users do not skip filling in important information.

We will look at how to make any fields of your choice required in this recipe, with field configurations. A field configuration controls the behavior of a field; this includes the field's mandatory requirements, visibility, renderer, and description.

How to do it...

Proceed with the following steps to make a field required in Jira:

1. Log into Jira with a user that has a Jira administrators permission.
2. Navigate to **Administration > Issues > Field Configurations.**
3. Click on the **Configure** link for the field configuration used by the project and issue type.
4. Click on the **Required** link for the field you want to make required, such as **Due Date.**

Once you have marked a field as required, such as **Due Date** in our case, whenever you create or edit an issue, Jira will make sure a value is entered for it, as shown in the following screenshot:

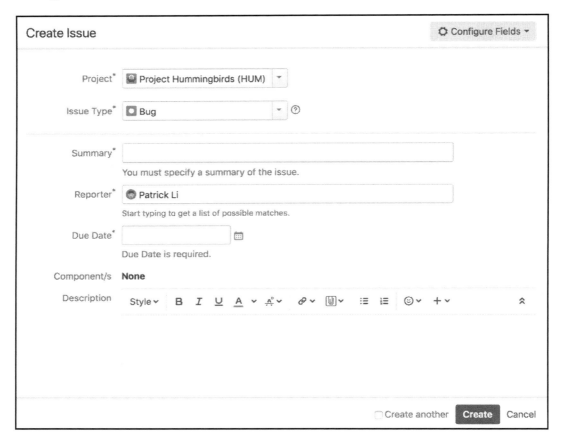

We will now have a look at how these steps work.

How it works...

When a field is marked as required, Jira will check to make sure that the field has a value when you are making updates to the issue, such as an edit, or during a workflow transition. This validation is applied even if the field is not present on the screen, so make sure you do not make a field that is not required on screen; otherwise, users will not be able to complete the action.

Certain fields, such as **Assignee** and **Due Date**, require the user to have certain permissions to make updates. If the user does not have the necessary permissions, the validation will fail, and prevent the user from completing the action.

There's more...

Clicking on the **Optional** link will make the field not required. Certain fields, such as **Summary** and **Issue Type**, must be required.

See also

Refer to the *Making the Assignee field required* recipe to see how to disable the unassigned option.

Making the Assignee field required

By default, the **Assignee** field has an unassigned option, which is equivalent to making the field optional. If you look at the field configuration, you will realize that you cannot make the **Assignee** field required, as there is no such option available.

In this recipe, we will look at how to disable the unassigned option, effectively making **Assignee** a required field.

Getting ready

Note the following conditions are required for your projects in order to disable the unassigned option for each individual project:

- Issues that are currently using that option for the **Assignee** field—you will need to change all issues with an **Unassigned** value for **Assignee** to something else.
- Projects that have **Unassigned** set as the default **Assignee**—you will need to change your project's **Default Assignee** setting in the **Users and roles** section.

How to do it...

Proceed with the following steps to disable the unassigned option:

1. Log into Jira with a user that has a Jira administrator's permission.
2. Navigate to **Administration** > **System.**
3. Click on the **Edit Settings** button.
4. Scroll down and select the **OFF** option for **Allow unassigned issues.**
5. Click on **Update** to apply the change.

Have a look at the following screenshot:

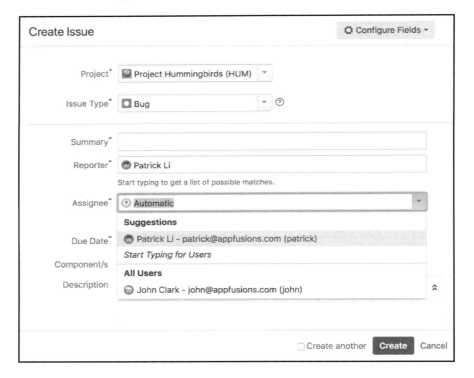

As you can see, once the option is disabled, issues can no longer be unassigned.

Hiding a field from view

There will be times when a field is no longer needed. When this happens, instead of deleting the field, which would also remove all its data, you can choose to hide it. If you need the field again further down the track, you can simply unhide it and retain all the data.

In this recipe, we will be hiding both the **Priority** and **Due Date** fields.

How to do it...

Proceed with the following steps to hide a field in Jira:

1. Log into Jira with a user that has a Jira administrator's permission.
2. Navigate to **Administration** > **Issues** > **Field Configurations.**
3. Click on the **Configure** link for the field configuration used by the project and issue type.
4. Click on the **Hide** link for **Priority** and **Due Date.**

Clicking on the **Show** link will expose the field. You should not hide a mandatory field.

There's more...

Using field configuration is one way to hide fields from the user. There are two more ways to make a field hidden from view:

- Take the field off screen. Note that for the **View** screen, default fields such as **Summary** and **Description** are shown regardless of whether or not they are placed on the screen.
- Restrict the field's configuration scheme so that it is not applicable to the project/issue type context. You can do this by clicking on the **Configure for the custom** field and deselecting the **project/issue** type you do not want the field to be available for.

Hiding the field with field configuration will make it hidden from all screens for the project and issue type it is applicable to, so, if you want to hide the field from specific screens, you should not use field configuration, but simply take the field off the appropriate screens. For example, if you want to make a field read-only after an issue is created, you can simply take it off the screen assigned to the edit issue operation. Pay close attention when you take fields off a screen; unlike field configurations, there are no safeguards in place to prevent you from taking a required field off a screen. So, if the screen is used for creating issues, then your users will be stuck, as they will not be able to provide a value for the required field that's missing from the screen.

Creating a new field configuration

You can configure a field's behavior with field configuration. Jira not only comes with a default field configuration that is applied to all project and issue types by default, but it also lets you create your own so that you can choose the projects and/or issue types to apply your field configuration to.

In this recipe, we will make the **Description** and **Assignee** fields required only for the **Bug** issue type.

How to do it...

Setting up a new field configuration is a three-step process. The first step is to create the new field configurations:

1. Log into Jira with a user that has a Jira administrator's permission.
2. Navigate to **Administration** > **Issues** > **Field Configurations.**
3. Click on the **Add Field Configuration** button, and name it HUM: Bug Field Configuration, and click on **Add.**
4. Click on the **Required** link for the **Description** and **Assignee** fields.

The second step is to associate the new field configuration with a new field configuration scheme:

1. Navigate to **Administration** > **Issues** > **Field configuration schemes**.
2. Click on the **Add field configuration scheme** button and name it HUM: Bug Field Configuration Scheme. Click on **Add**.
3. Click on the **Associate an issue type with a field configuration** button.

4. Select **Bug** for **Issue Type**, **HUM: Bug Field Configuration** for **Field Configuration**, and click on **Add**, as shown in the following screenshot:

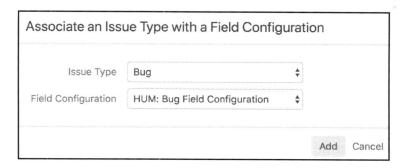

The last step is to apply the new field configuration scheme to our project:

1. Navigate to **Administration** > **Projects.**
2. Select a project from the list.
3. Select **Fields** from the left-hand panel.
4. Navigate to **Actions** > **Use a different scheme.**
5. Select the new HUM: Bug Field Configuration Scheme option and click on **Associate.**

Setting up customized screens for your project

Jira comes with three screens by default—the **Default** screen, the **Resolve Issue** screen, and the **Workflow** screen.

In this recipe, we will look at how to create a new screen from scratch, and then make it appear when we are creating a new Task issue.

How to do it...

The screen is one of the most complicated configurations in Jira. To create a new screen and apply it often requires you to configure multiple schemes. So, we will break these steps into three logical groups.

Firstly, we need to create our new screen:

1. Log into Jira with a user that has a Jira administrator's permission.
2. Navigate to **Administration** > **Issues** > **Screens**.
3. Click on the **Add Screen** button and name the new screen HUM: Scrum Task Create Screen. Click on **Add**.
4. Select and add the **Summary**, **Issue Type**, **Description**, **Assignee**, **Description**, and **Priority** fields, as shown in the following screenshot:

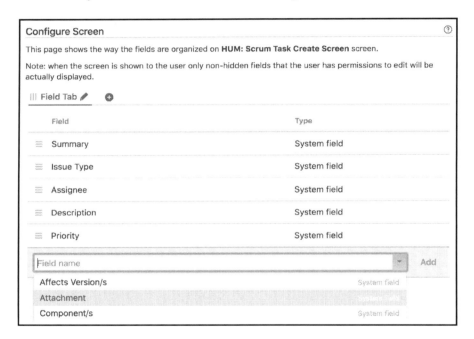

Secondly, we need to assign the new **Task Create Screen** to the **Create Issue** operation:

1. Navigate to **Administration** > **Issues** > **Screen schemes**.
2. Click on the **Add Screen Scheme** button, name the new screen HUM: Scrum Task Screen Scheme, select **Default Screen** as the **Default Screen** option, and click on **Add**.
3. Click on the **Associate an Issue Operation with a Screen** button.
4. Select **Create Issue** for **Issue Operation**, **HUM: Scrum Task Create Screen** for **Screen**, and click on **Add**, as shown in the following screenshot:

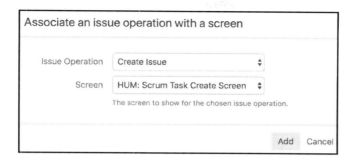

Third, we need to assign the new `Task Screen Scheme` to the **Task** issue type:

1. Navigate to **Administration** > **Issues** > **Issue type screen schemes**.
2. Click on the **Add Issue Type Screen Scheme** button and name the new screen `HUM: Scrum Task Issue Type Screen Scheme`.
3. Select the **Default Screen Scheme** as the **Screen Scheme** option and click on **Add**.
4. Click on the **Associate an issue Type with a Screen Scheme** button.
5. Select **Task** for **Issue Type**, **HUM: Scrum Task Screen Scheme** for **Screen Scheme**, and click on **Add**, as shown in the following screenshot:

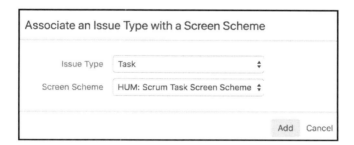

Lastly, we need to apply the new screen `Task Issue Type Screen Scheme` to the project:

1. Navigate to **Administration** > **Projects**.
2. Select a project from the list.
3. Select **Screens** from the left-hand pane.
4. Navigate to **Actions** > **Use a different scheme**.
5. Select the new **Task Issue Type Screen Scheme** and click on **Associate**.

How it works...

The screen is one of the most intricate aspects of Jira configuration. When we create a new screen, we need to associate it with one of the three issue operations (create, edit, and view) with a screen scheme. In our recipe, we associated our new **Task Create Screen** with the **Create Issue** operation.

Screen schemes then need to be associated with issue types, so that Jira can determine which screen scheme to use, based on the selected issue type.

Lastly, we apply the **Issue Type Screen Scheme** to a project, so only the selected projects will have the associated screens. Now take a look at the following diagram:

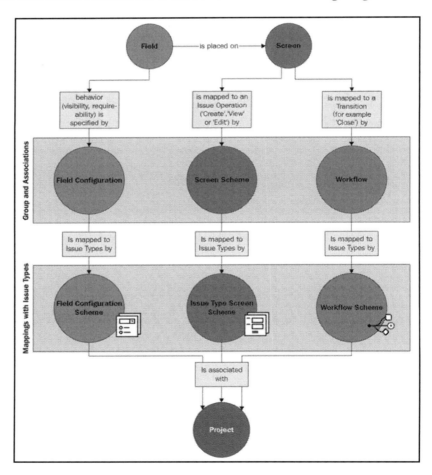

It provides a comprehensive illustration of the relationships between screens, fields, and their various schemes.

Removing a select list's None option

Custom field types such as select list (single and multi) come with the **None** option, and the only way to remove it is to make the field required. While this makes sense, it can be cumbersome to chase down every field and configuration.

In this recipe, we will remove the **None** option from all single select list custom fields.

Getting ready

Since we will be modifying physical files in Jira, you will want to take backups of the files we change.

How to do it...

Jira uses Velocity templates to render custom fields. These templates are mostly HTML, with some special symbols. You can find all these files in the `JIRA_INSTALL/atlassian-jira/WEB-INF/classes/templates/plugins/fields` directory, and the edit view templates are in the `edit` subdirectory:

1. Open the `edit-select.vm` file (located in the previously mentioned directory) in a text editor, and remove the following code snippet:

```
#if (!$fieldLayoutItem || $fieldLayoutItem.required ==  false)
 <option value="-1">
  $i18n.getText("common.words.none")
 </option>
#else
 #if ( !$configs.default )
  <option value="">
   $i18n.getText("common.words.none")
  </option>
 #end
#end
```

2. Save the file and restart Jira. Make sure you do not change any other lines.

 You can remove the **None** option from other custom field types, such as multi-select, by editing the appropriate file (for example, `edit-multiselect.vm`).

How it works...

The Velocity `.vm` template files are what Jira uses to render the HTML for the custom fields. The code snippet we removed is what displays the **None** option. Note that, by changing the template, we are removing the **None** option for all single select custom fields in Jira. If you just want to remove the **None** option for a single custom field or only for certain projects, refer to the *Using JavaScript with custom fields* recipe.

Adding help tips to custom fields

Users who are new to Jira often find it confusing when it comes to filling in fields, especially custom fields. Therefore, it is for you as the administrator to provide useful tips and descriptions to explain what some of the fields are for.

In this recipe, we will be adding a help icon to a customer field that we have called **Team**. You can apply this recipe to any custom fields you have in your Jira.

How to do it...

Proceed with the following steps to add help tips to a custom field:

1. Log into Jira with a user that has a Jira administrator's permission.
2. Navigate to **Administration > Issues > Custom Fields**.
3. Click on the **Edit** link for the custom field.
4. Enter the following HTML snippet into the **Description** text box, and click on **Update**. You might want to substitute the `href` value to a real page containing help text:

```
Need help to work out assignment?
<a class="help-lnk"
href="/secure/ShowConstantsHelp.jspa?decorator=popup#Teams"
```

```
data-helplink="local" target="_blank">
    <span class="aui-icon aui-icon-small aui-iconfont-
help"></span>
    </a>
```

The following screenshot shows our new help icon:

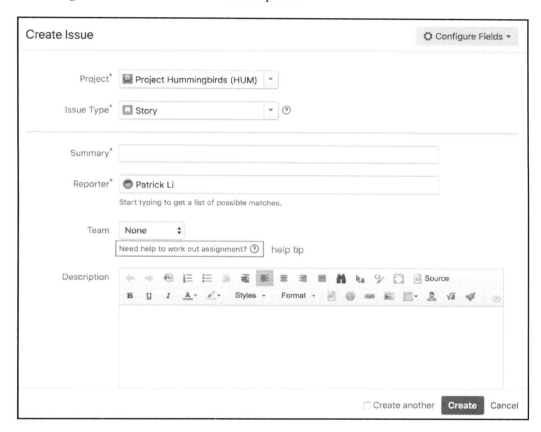

We will now go through how these steps work.

How it works...

Jira allows us to use any valid HTML for custom field description, so we added some simple text and an `anchor` tag that links to an HTML page containing our help information. We also added a `span` tag with the proper style class in order to have the nice question mark icon used by the **Issue Type** and **Priority** fields.

The `data-helplink="local"` attribute for the `anchor` tag ensures that, when the user clicks on the help icon, the help page is opened in a separate page rather than redirecting the current page.

 Since the custom field description is rendered as it is, make sure you validate your HTML; for example, close all your HTML tags.

There's more...

Normally, we put descriptions directly into the custom field's description textbox, as demonstrated. You can also put your descriptions into the field configuration settings, such as hiding a field. Doing so offers the following advantages:

- You can have different help text for different project/issue type contexts.
- You can set help text for fields that are not custom fields, such as **Summary** and **Description**.

Proceed with the following steps to set field descriptions in the field configuration:

1. Navigate to **Administration** > **Issues** > **Field Configurations**.
2. Click on the **Configure** link for the field configuration used by the project and issue type.
3. Click on the **Edit** link for the field.
4. Enter the HTML snippets into the **Description** field, and click on **Update**.

See also

Refer to the *Using JavaScript with custom fields* recipe for other tricks you can do with custom field descriptions.

Using JavaScript with custom fields

JavaScript can be used to manipulate the HTML of custom fields. By adding JavaScript code in the custom field description and wrapping the code in <script> tags, Jira will execute the code when the custom field is rendered.

In this recipe, we will look at another way of removing the **None** option from select list custom fields.

Getting ready

This recipe uses the jQuery JavaScript library, which is bundled with Jira. If you are not familiar with jQuery, you can find the documentation at http://jquery.com.

We will also need to use the custom field's ID in our script, so you will need to have that handy. You can find the ID by going to the **Custom fields** page, clicking on the **Edit** link of the target field, and clicking the number at the end of the URL, which is the field's ID. For example, the following URL shows a custom field with the ID 10103:

http://jira.localhost.com:8080/secure/admin/EditCustomField!default.jsp
a?id=10103

How to do it...

Proceed with the following steps to add JavaScript to custom field description:

1. Log into Jira with a user that has a Jira administrator's permission.
2. Navigate to **Administration** > **Issues** > **Custom Fields**.
3. Click on the **Edit** link for the custom field.
4. Enter the following JavaScript snippet into the **Description** text box, and click on **Update**. You will need to substitute it in your custom field's ID:

```
<script>
 AJS.$('#customfield_10103 option[value="-  1"]').remove();
</script>
```

The following screenshot shows that the **Team** custom field:

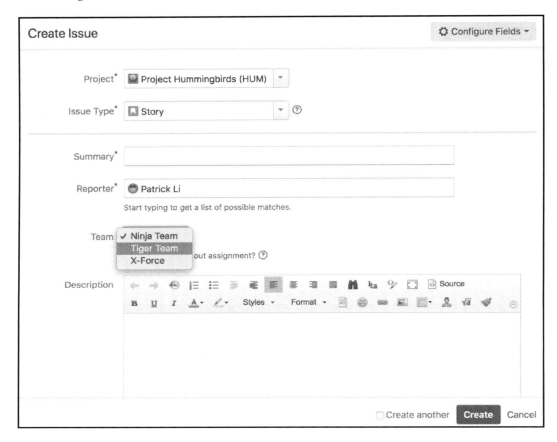

As you can see, the **None** option is no longer available.

How it works...

In our script, we use jQuery to select the **Team** custom field, based on its element ID, and remove the option with the value –1 (which is the **None** option) with the `#customfield_10103 option[value="-1"]` selector.

We use the **Atlassian JavaScript** (**AJS**) namespace (`AJS.$`), which is the recommended way to use jQuery in Jira.

Setting default values for fields

As you add more and more fields onto your screens, sometimes it can be overwhelming and confusing for your end users, especially for free text fields such as **Description**. Users will often enter data however they like. To help with that, one way is to have instructions set as default values for some of these fields to help guide your users with their inputs. For those of you who have used other systems, such as GitHub, this is a common practice.

In this recipe, we will look at how to set up a default value for the **Description** field, in the form of instructions for users to follow when creating a bug report.

Getting ready

For this recipe, we need to have the ScriptRunner for Jira add-on installed. You can download it from the following link, or install it directly from the Universal Plugin Manager at `https://marketplace.atlassian.com/plugins/com.onresolve.jira.groovy.groovyrunner`.

You may also want to get familiar with Groovy scripting at `http://groovy-lang.org`.

How to do it...

Once you have installed the ScriptRunner for Jira add-on, we will first need to create what is known as a behavior:

1. Log into Jira with a user that has a Jira administrator's permission.
2. Navigate to **Administration > Manage apps > Behaviors.**
3. Create a new behavior by entering a name for it and clicking the **Add** button.

With the new behavior created, we need to first create a mapping, so Jira will know what to apply the behavior to:

1. Click on the **Add Mapping** link of the new behavior we have created.
2. Select **All projects** and **Bug** issue type for our mapping.
3. Click the **Add Mapping** button to save the setting.

With the mapping created, we can now start setting default values:

1. Click on the **Fields** link of the new behavior we have created.
2. Click on the **Create initialiser** link:

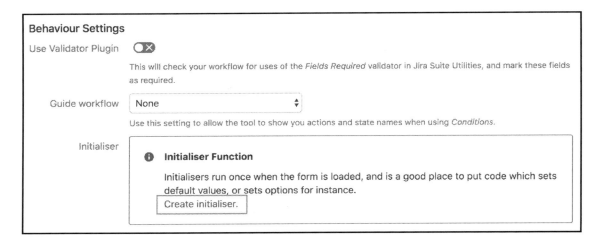

3. Enter the following code into the text editor:

```
1.      def desc = getFieldById("description")
2.      def defaultValue = ""
3.      h2. Describe the problem
4.      Tell us in details what the problem you are having.
5.
6.      h2. How to reproduce
7.      List out the steps to reproduce the problem.
8.      * step 1
9.      * step 2
10.
11.     h2. Expected Result
12.     Tell us what you think the correct outcome should be after
completing the steps 13.    listed above.
14.
15.     h2. Actual Result
16.     Tell us what you actually see after completing the steps
listed above."""
17.
18.     if (!underlyingIssue?.description) {
19.         desc.setFormValue(defaultValue)
20.     }
```

4. Click on **Save** to save our changes.

Now, if you try to create a new **Bug** issue, you should see the **Description** field pre-populated with our default value, as shown here:

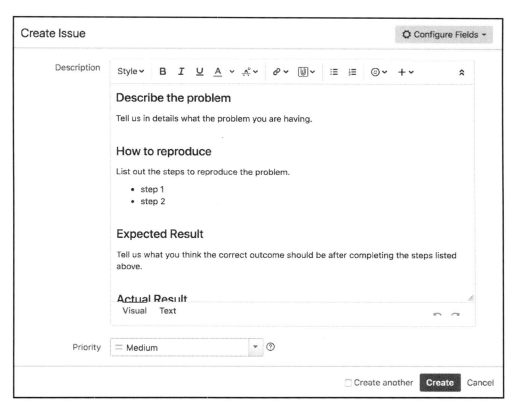

We will now go have a look at how the steps work.

How it works...

Our code is written in Groovy, which is very similar to Java, the technology used by Jira. We first try to get hold of the `Description` field in line #1, and, from line #3 to #20, we use wiki markup, the markup language used by Jira's out-of-the-box editor, to create your default value in the form of instructions. On line #18, we check whether the issue already has a description value set, such as user-entered content, and, if not, we will apply our default value on line #19.

Adding permission to fields

Out of the box, Jira comes with several levels of permissions, starting at the system level and going down to the issue level, allowing you to control who should have access to issues. While this is usually sufficient, you will find yourself needing to apply permissions to individual fields. For example, you may want a field such as **Description** to be read-only for everyone, but only editable by a select group of users.

One option is to create your own custom field types, as described in the later recipe, and code the permission requirement as part of the field, but this approach requires programming and cannot be applied to fields that are not created by you.

In this recipe, we will look at an option to apply field-level permissions to both system fields and custom fields.

Getting ready

For this recipe, we need to have the ScriptRunner for Jira add-on installed. You can download it from the following link, or install it directly from the Universal Plugin Manager at `https://marketplace.atlassian.com/plugins/com.onresolve.jira.groovy.groovyrunner`.

How to do it...

Once you have installed the ScriptRunner for Jira add-on, we will first need to create what is known as a behavior:

1. Log into Jira with a user that has a Jira administrator's permission.
2. Navigate to **Administration** > **Manage apps** > **Behaviors.**
3. Create a new behavior by entering a name for it and clicking the **Add** button.

With the new behavior created, we need to first create a mapping, so Jira will know what to apply the behavior to:

1. Click on the **Add Mapping** link of the new behavior we have created.
2. Select the projects and issue types you want to apply the behavior to. If you want this to be global, you can select the **All projects** and **All issue types** options.
3. Click the **Add Mapping** button to save the setting.

With the mapping created, we can now start setting our field-level permission behaviors:

1. Click on the **Fields** link of the new behavior we have created.
2. Select the fields you want to apply field-level permissions to.
3. Toggle the available behavior options on and off, as shown here:

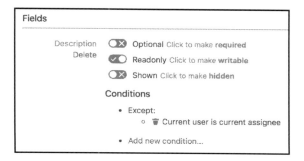

4. Click on the **Add new condition** link and select which users the permission should be applied to. In the following screenshot, the permission will be applied to everyone except users in the `jira-administrators` group:

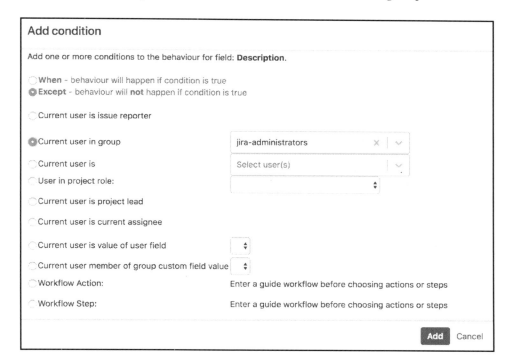

5. Click on the **Add** button to add the condition.
6. After you are done with adding fields and conditions, click on the **Save** button.

Once we have created and configured our field-level permissions, the changes will be applied immediately to the target issues according to the mappings we have configured. Have a look at the next screenshot:

As you can see, the **Description** field (a system field) and the **Team** field (a custom field) are in read-only mode when a user is editing the issue.

Creating your own custom field types

All custom fields that come out-of-the-box with Jira have predefined purposes, such as the text field, which allows users to type in some simple text. It will often be useful to have a specialized custom field that does exactly what you need. Unfortunately, this often requires custom development efforts.

However, there is an add-on that provides a custom field type that lets you use Groovy scripts to power its logic.

In this recipe, we will look at how to create a custom field that uses a Groovy script to display the total number of comments on any given issue.

Getting ready

For this recipe, we need to have the ScriptRunner for Jira add-on installed. You can download it from the following link, or install it directly from the Universal Plugin Manager at `https://marketplace.atlassian.com/plugins/com.onresolve.jira.groovy.groovyrunner`.

You may also want to get familiar with Groovy scripting at `http://groovy-lang.org`.

How to do it...

Creating a scripted field is a two-step process. We first need to create an instance of the custom field in Jira, and then add the script to it:

1. Log into Jira with a user that has a Jira administrator's permission.
2. Navigate to **Administration** > **Issues** > **Custom fields**.
3. Click on the **Add Custom Field** button and select **Advanced** from the dialog box.

4. Scroll down and select **Scripted Field** from the list; click on **Next**, as shown in the following screenshot:

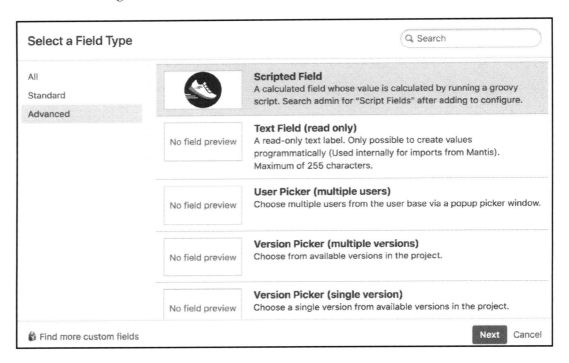

5. Name our new custom field `Total Comments` and add it to the appropriate screens.
6. Navigate to **Administration** > **Manage apps** > **Script Fields**.
7. Select the **Edit** option for the `Total Comments` field.
8. Enter the following Groovy script in the script text box:

```
import com.atlassian.jira.component.ComponentAccessor
import com.atlassian.jira.issue.comments.CommentManager

def commentManager = ComponentAccessor.getCommentManager()
def numberOfComments = commentManager.getComments(issue).size()

return numberOfComments ? numberOfComments as Double : null
```

9. Select **Number Field** for **Template** and click on **Update**, as shown in the following screenshot:

When the custom field is added to an issue, it will automatically calculate the number of comments the issue has in real time, as shown in the following screenshot:

Now it's time to look to understand the steps.

How it works...

The scripted field type is an example of what is called the calculated custom field type. The calculated custom field type is a special custom field that derives (calculates) its value based on some predefined logic, in this case, our Groovy script. Every time the field is displayed, Jira will recalculate the field's value so it is always kept up to date.

Jira Workflows 3

Workflows are one of the core and most powerful features in Jira. They control how issues in Jira move from one stage to another as they are being worked on, sometimes being re-assigned to other users and capturing additional information during the process. For this reason, workflows can be thought of as the life cycle of issues.

Unlike many other systems, Jira allows you to create your own workflows to resemble the work processes you may already have in your organization. This is a good example of how Jira is able to adapt to your needs without you having to change the way you work.

In this chapter, we will learn not only about how to create workflows with the new workflow designer, but also how to use workflow components, such as conditions and validators, to add additional behavior to your workflows. We will also look at the many different apps that are available to expand the possibilities of what you can do with workflows.

In this chapter, we will cover the following recipes:

- Setting up different workflows for your project
- Capturing additional information during workflow transitions
- Using common transitions
- Using global transitions
- Restricting the availability of workflow transitions

- Validating user input in workflow transitions
- Performing additional processing after a transition is executed
- Reacting to events coming from outside of Jira
- Rearranging the workflow transition bar
- Restricting the resolution values in a transition
- Preventing issue updates in selected statuses
- Making a field required during a workflow transition
- Creating custom workflow transition logic

Setting up different workflows for your project

A workflow is like a flowchart in which issues can go from one state to another by following the direction paths between the states. In Jira's workflow terminology, the states are called **statuses**, and the paths are called **transitions**. We will use these two major components when customizing a workflow.

In this recipe, we will create a new, simple workflow from scratch. We will look at how to use existing statuses, create new statuses, and link them together using transitions.

How to do it...

The first step is to create a new skeleton workflow in Jira:

1. Log into Jira with a user that has a Jira Administrator's permission.
2. Navigate to **Administration > Issues > Workflows.**
3. Click on the **Add workflow** button, and name the workflow `Simple Workflow`.
4. Click on the **Diagram** button to use the workflow designer or diagram mode.

The following screenshot explains some of the key elements of the workflow designer:

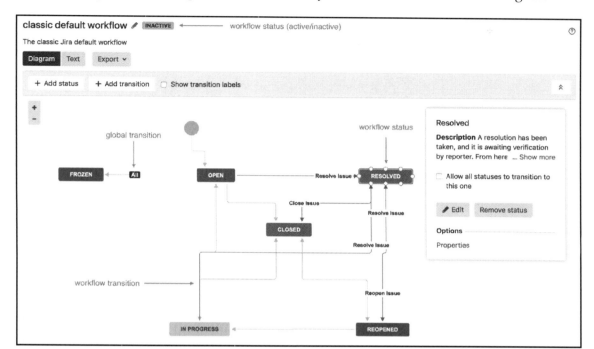

Now we have created a new, inactive workflow. The next step is to add various statuses for the issues to go through. Jira comes with a number of existing statuses, such as **In Progress** and **Resolved**, for us to use:

1. Click on the **Add status** button.
2. Select the **In Progress** status from the list, and click on **Add.**
3. Repeat the steps to add the **Closed** status.

You can type the status name into the field, and Jira will automatically find the status for you.

Once you have added the statuses to the workflow, you can drag them around to reposition them on the canvas. We can also create new statuses, as follows:

1. Click on the **Add status** button.

2. Name the new status `Frozen`, check the **Allow all statuses to transition to this one** option, and click on **Add**, as shown in the following screenshot:

 Jira will let you know if the status you are entering is new by showing the text (**new status**) next to the status name.

Now that we have added the statuses, we need to link them using transitions:

1. Select the originating status, which, in this example, is **OPEN**.
2. Click on the small circle around the **OPEN** status and drag your cursor onto the **IN PROGRESS** status. This will prompt you to provide details for the new transition, as shown in the following screenshot:

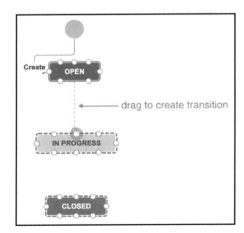

3. Name the new transition `Start Progress`, and select the **None** option for the screen.
4. Repeat the steps to create a transition called `Close` between the **IN PROGRESS** and **CLOSED** statuses.

You should finish with a workflow that looks like the following screenshot:

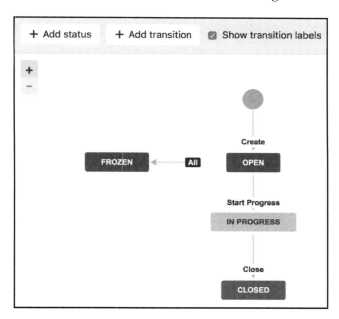

At this point, the workflow is inactive, which means it is not being used by a project and you can edit it without any restrictions. Workflows are applied on a project and issue type basis. Perform the following steps to apply the new workflow to a project:

1. Select the project to apply the workflow to.
2. Click on the **Administration** tab to go to the project administration page.
3. Select **Workflows** from the left-hand side of the page.
4. Click on **Add Existing** from the **Add Workflow** menu.
5. Select the new **Simple Workflow** from the dialog, and click on **Next**.
6. Choose the issue types to apply (for example, **Bug**) the workflow to, and click on **Finish**.

After we have applied the workflow to a project, the workflow is placed in the active state. So, if we now create a new issue in the target project of the selected issue type, our new **Simple Workflow** will be used.

Capturing additional information during workflow transitions

When users execute a workflow transition, we have an option to display an intermediate workflow screen. This is a very useful way of collecting some additional information from the user. For example, the default Jira workflow will display a screen for users to select the **Resolution** value when the issue is resolved.

 Issues with resolution values are considered completed. You should only add the **Resolution** field to workflow screens that represent the closing of an issue.

Getting ready

We need to have a workflow to configure, such as the **Simple Workflow** that was created in the previous recipe. We also need to have screens to display; Jira's out-of-the-box workflow screen and **Result Issue Screen** will suffice, but if you have created your own screens, they can also be used.

How to do it...

Perform the following steps to add a screen to a workflow transition:

1. Select the workflow to update, such as our **Simple Workflow**.
2. Click on the **Edit** button if the workflow is active. This will create a draft workflow for us to work on.
3. Select the **Start Progress** transition, and click on the **Edit** link from the panel on the right-hand side.
4. Select the screen you want to use, such as the workflow screen from the **Screen** drop-down menu, and click on **Save**.
5. Repeat *step 3* and *step 4* to add **Resolve Issue Screen** to the **Close** transition.

If we are working with a draft workflow, we must click on the **Publish Draft** button to apply our changes to the live workflow.

> If you do not see your changes reflected, it is most likely you forgot to publish your draft workflow.

Using common transitions

Often, you will have transitions that need to be made available from several different statuses in a workflow, such as the **Resolve** and **Close** transitions. In other words, these are transitions that have a common destination status but many different originating statuses.

To help you simplify the process of creating these transitions, Jira lets you reuse an existing transition as a common transition if it has the same destination status.

> Common transitions are transitions that have the same destination status but different originating statuses.

A common transition has an additional advantage of ensuring that transition screens and other relevant configurations, such as **validators**, will stay consistent. Otherwise, you will have to constantly check the various transitions every time you make a change to one of them.

How to do it...

Perform the following steps to create and use common transitions in your workflow:

1. Select the workflow, and click on the **Edit** link to create a draft.
2. Select the **Diagram** mode.
3. Create a transition between two statuses, for example, **Open** and **Closed**.

4. Create another transition from a different status to the same destination status, and click on the **Reuse a transition** tab, as seen in the following screenshot:

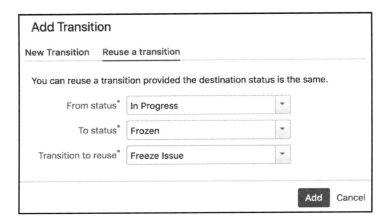

5. Select the transition created in *step 3* from the **Transition to reuse** drop-down menu, and click on **Add**.
6. Click on **Publish Draft** to apply the change.

See also

Refer to the *Using global transitions* recipe, which helps us to create complicated workflows with ease by allowing an issue to transition into a status at any time.

Using global transitions

While a common transition is a great way to share transitions in a workflow and reduce the amount of management work that would otherwise be required, it has the limitation of having to manually create the transitions between the various statuses.

As your workflow starts becoming more complicated, explicitly creating the transitions becomes a tedious job; this is where **global transitions** come in.

A global transition is similar to a common transition in the sense that they both share the property of having a single destination status. The difference between the two is that the global transition is a single transition that is available to all the statuses in a workflow.

In this recipe, we will look at how to use global transitions so that issues can be transitioned to the **Frozen** status from any status throughout the workflow.

Getting ready

As usual, you need to have a workflow you can edit. Since we will be demonstrating how global transitions work, you need to have a status called **Frozen** in your workflow and ensure that there are no transitions linked to it.

How to do it...

Perform the following steps to create and use global transitions in your workflow:

1. Select and edit the workflow you will be adding the global transition to.
2. Select **Diagram** mode.
3. Select the **Frozen**status.
4. Check the **Allow all statuses to transition to this one** option.
5. Click on **Publish Draft** to apply the change.

The following screenshot depicts the preceding steps:

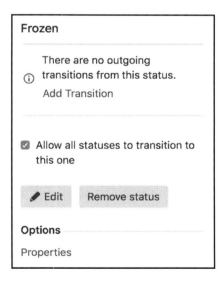

6. Once you have created a global transition for a status, it will be represented as an **All** transition, as shown in the following screenshot:

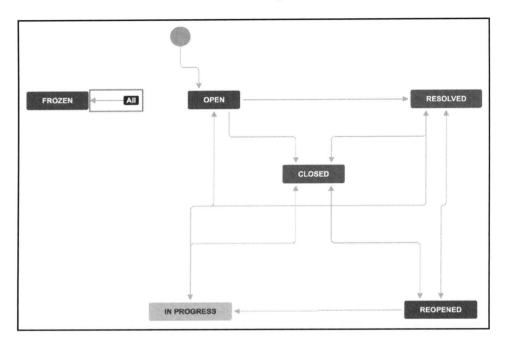

After the global transition is added to the **Frozen** status, you will be able to transition issues to **FROZEN** regardless of their current status.

 You can only add global transitions in **Diagram** mode.

See also

Refer to the *Restricting the availability of workflow transitions* recipe, which explains how to remove a transition when an issue is already in the **Frozen** status.

Restricting the availability of workflow transitions

Workflow transitions, by default, are accessible to anyone who has access to the issue. There will be times when you want to restrict access to certain transitions. For example, you might want to restrict access to the **Freeze Issue** transition for the following reasons:

- You want the transition to be available only to users in specific groups or project roles.
- Since the transition is a global transition, it is available to all the workflow statuses, but it does not make sense to show the transition when the issue is already in the **Frozen** status.

To restrict the availability of a workflow transition, we can use workflow conditions.

Getting ready

For this recipe, we need to have the JSU Automation Suite for Jira Workflows app installed. You can download it from the following link, or install it directly from the **Universal Plugin Manager** (**UPM**): https://marketplace.atlassian.com/plugins/com.googlecode. jira-suite-utilities.

How to do it...

We need to add a new workflow condition to the transition we want to apply restrictions to:

1. Select and edit the workflow to configure.
2. Select **Diagram** mode.
3. Click on the **Frozen** global workflow transition.
4. Click on the **Conditions** link from the panel on the right-hand side.
5. Click on **Add condition**, select **Value Field (JSU)** from the list, and click on **Add**.
6. Configure the condition with the following parameters:
    - The Status field for **Field**
    - The not-equal sign, !=, for **Condition**
    - Frozen for **Value**
    - String for **Comparison Type**

This means that the transition will be shown only if the issue's status field value is not **Frozen** as shown in the following screenshot:

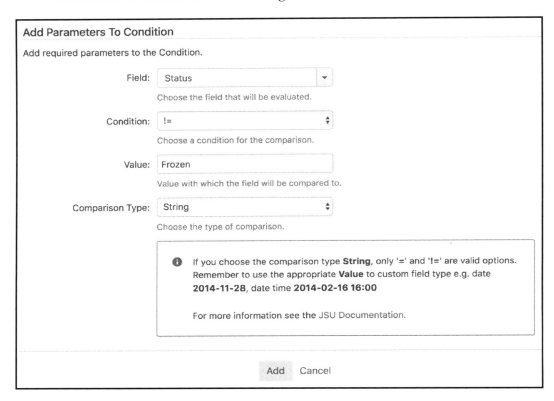

7. Click on the **Add** button to complete the condition setup.

   At this point, we have added a condition that will make sure that the **Freeze Issue** transition is not shown when the issue is already in the **Frozen** status. The next step is to add another condition to restrict the transition to be available only to users in the **Developer** role.

8. Click on **Add condition** again and select **User in the Project Role** condition.
9. Select the **Developer** project role and click on **Add**.
10. Click on **Publish Draft** to apply the change.

After you have applied the workflow conditions, the **Frozen** transition will no longer be available if the issue is already in the **Frozen** status, and/or if the current user is not in the **Developer** project role.

How it works...

When a workflow transition option is to be rendered on the page, such as when viewing an issue, all its associated conditions are evaluated to determine if the option should be displayed. If there is more than one condition, the transition with conditions will only be displayed when one or all of the conditions pass, depending on the logic setting (see the following section) for the conditions.

There's more...

Using the Value Field condition (which comes with the JSU Automation Suite for Jira Workflows app) is one of the many ways in which we can restrict the availability of a transition based on the issue's current status. There is another app, called **Jira Misc Workflow Extensions**, which comes with a previous status condition for checking against the previous status an issue was in. You can download it from `https://marketplace.` `atlassian.com/plugins/com.innovalog.jmwe.jira-misc-workflow-extensions`.

When you have more than one workflow condition applied to the transition, as in our example, the default behavior is that all conditions must pass for the transition to be available.

You can change this so that only one condition needs to pass for the transition to be available by changing the condition group logic from **All of the following conditions** to **Any of the following conditions**, as shown in the following screenshot:

Make sure you pay close attention when configuring this to make sure you do not expose workflow transitions to users who should not be allowed to execute them.

Validating user input in workflow transitions

For workflow transitions that have transition screens, you can add validation logic to make sure what the users put in is what you are expecting. This is a great way to ensure data integrity, and we can do this with workflow validators.

In this recipe, we will add a validator to perform a date comparison between a custom field and the issue's creation date, so the date value we select for the custom field must be after the issue's creation date.

Getting ready

For this recipe, we need to have the JSU Automation Suite for Jira Workflows app installed. You can download it from the following link, or install it directly using the UPM: `https://marketplace.atlassian.com/plugins/com.googlecode.jira-suite-utilities`.

Since we are also doing a date comparison, we need to create a new date custom field called `Start Date` and add it to the workflow screen.

How to do it...

Perform the following steps to add validation rules during a workflow transition:

1. Select and edit the workflow to configure.
2. Select the **Diagram** mode.
3. Select the **Start Progress** transition and click on the **Validators** link on the right-hand side.
4. Click on the **Add validator** link and select **Date Compare (JSU)** from the list.
5. Configure the validator with the following parameters:
    - The `Start Date` custom field for **This date.**
    - The greater-than sign, >, for **Condition**
    - `Created` for **Compare with**
    - An optional custom error message, or leave it blank and a default error message will be displayed if the validation fails

6. Click on **Add** to add the validator:

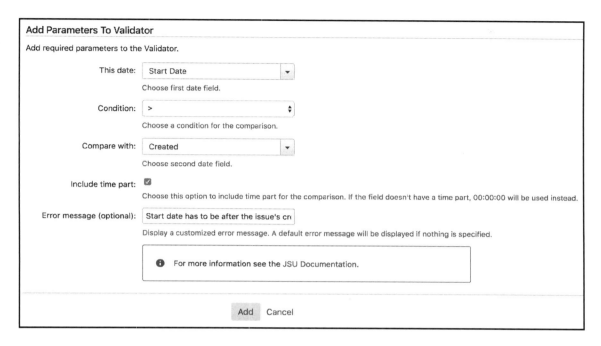

7. Click on **Publish Draft** to apply the change.

After adding the validator, if we now try to select a date that is before the issue's create date, Jira will prompt you with an error message and stop the transition from going through, as shown in the following screenshot:

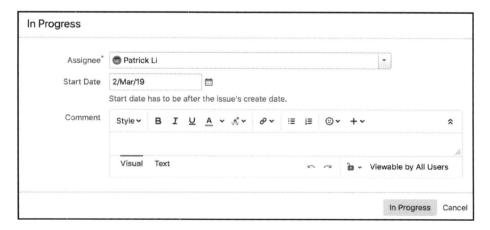

As we can see, the date validation fails, and our custom defined error message is displayed.

How it works...

Validators are run before the workflow transition is executed. This way, validators can intercept and prevent a transition from going through if any validation logic fails.

 If you have more than one validator, all of them must pass for the transition to go through.

See also

Validators can be used to make a field required only during workflow transitions. Refer to the *Making a field required during a workflow transition* recipe for more details.

Performing additional processing after a transition is executed

Jira allows you to perform additional tasks as part of a workflow transition through the use of post functions. Jira makes heavy use of post functions internally; for example, in the case of an out-of-the-box workflow, the resolution field value is cleared automatically when you reopen an issue.

In this recipe, we will look at how to add post functions to a workflow transition. We will add a post function to automatically clear out the value stored in a **Reason for Freezing** custom field when we take it out of the **Frozen** status.

Getting ready

Since we are clearing the value of a custom field called **Reason for Freezing**, we need to have a **Text** field (multi-line) custom field created and add it to the screens used by the project.

By default, Jira comes with a post function that can change the values for standard issue fields, but since **Reason for Freezing** will be a custom field, we need to have the JSU Automation Suite for Jira Workflows app installed.

You can download it from the following link, or install it directly using the UPM: `https://marketplace.atlassian.com/plugins/com.googlecode.jira-suite-utilities`.

How to do it...

Perform the following steps to add processing logic after a workflow transition is executed:

1. Select and edit the workflow to configure.
2. Select the **Diagram** mode.
3. Create a new workflow transition that will take the issue out of the **Frozen** status to another status.
4. Click on the **Post functions** link for the newly created transition.
5. Click on **Add post function**, select **Clear Field Value (JSU)** from the list, and click on **Add**.
6. Select the **Reason for Freezing** field from **Field**, and click on the **Add** button.
7. Click on **Publish Draft** to apply the change.

With the post function in place, after you have executed the transition, the **Reason for Freezing** field will be cleared out. You can also see from the issue's change history, as part of the transition execution, where the **Status** field is changed from **Frozen** to **Open**, the change for the **Reason for Freezing** field is also recorded.

How it works...

Post functions are run after the transition has been executed. When you add a new post function, you might notice that the transition already has a number of post functions pre-added; this is shown in the screenshot that follows:

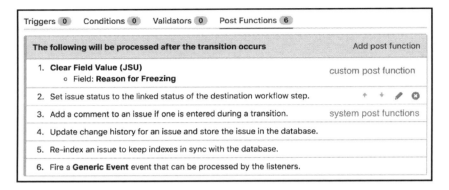

These post functions are system post functions that carry out important internal functions, such as keeping the search index up to date. The order of these post functions is important.

 Always add your own post functions to the top of the list.

For example, any changes to issue field values, such as the one we just added, should always happen before the **Re-index** post function, so by the time the transition is completed, all the field indexes are up to date, and ready to be searched:

Reacting to events coming from outside of Jira

When you are using Jira with other systems, especially applications also built by Atlassian, such as Bitbucket and Bamboo, you can get a lot more synergy with them working together. One example of such synergy is automatically executing a workflow transition when certain actions happen from the other application.

In this recipe, we will look at such a use case, where if a developer commits some code against a Jira issue, we automatically transition the issue into the **In Progress** status without needing the developer to manually go into Jira and perform the workflow transition.

Getting ready

Since our use case is about developers committing code, you will need to have a supported code management application available; both Bitbucket and GitHub are supported. In this recipe, we will be using Bitbucket. You can get a trial version of the application from `https://www.atlassian.com/software/bitbucket/download`.

How to do it...

To automatically transition an issue based on the outside event, we need to add the appropriate workflow trigger to the transition:

1. Select and edit the workflow to configure.
2. Select the **Start Progress** transition.
3. Click on the **Triggers** button.
4. Click on the **Add trigger** button. If the button is disabled, it means you have not integrated Jira with Bitbucket yet.
5. Select the **Commit created** trigger and click **Next**:

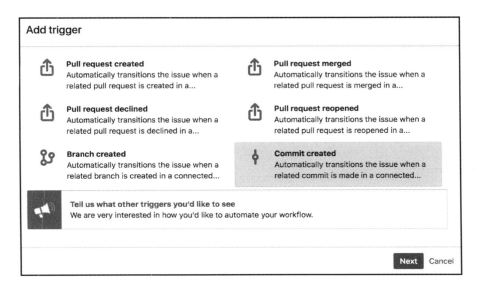

6. Click **Add Trigger** to apply the trigger to the workflow transition.

7. Click on **Publish Draft** to apply the change.

With the trigger applied, if you commit some code with the issue's key as part of the commit message, the issue will be automatically transitioned to the destination status, in this case, the **In Progress** status.

Rearranging the workflow transition bar

By default, workflow transitions are displayed based in the order in which they are defined in the workflow (as listed in text mode); the first two transitions will be shown as buttons, and the remaining transitions will be added to the **Workflow** menu.

This sequence is determined by the order in which the transitions are added, so you cannot change that. But you can rearrange them by using the `opsbar-sequence` property.

In this recipe, we will move the **Frozen** transition out from the **Workflow** menu and to its own transition button so that the users can easily access it.

How to do it...

Perform the following steps to rearrange the order of transitions to be displayed in the issue transition bar:

1. Select and edit the workflow to configure.

2. Select the **Frozen** global transition.

3. Click on the **Properties** button.

4. Enter `opsbar-sequence` as the **Property Key** and the value 10 in **Property Value** and click on **Add**. Click on **Publish Draft** to apply the change.

As shown in the following screenshot, by increasing the sequence value of the workflow transition, it is moved out of the **Workflow** menu and made into its own button:

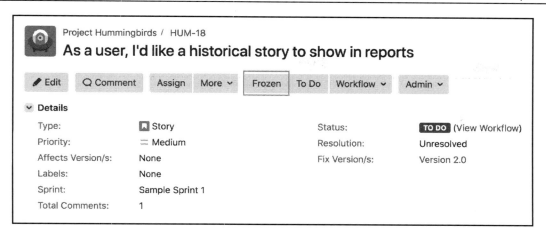

Now let's understand the working part.

How it works...

The `opsbar-sequence` property orders the workflow transitions numerically, from the smallest to the largest. Its value needs to be a positive integer. The smaller the number, the closer the transition will appear to the front.

There's more...

Jira only displays the first two transitions as buttons. You can change this setting by editing the `ops.bar.group.size.opsbar-transitions` property in the `jira-config.properties` file located in your JIRA_HOME directory.

All you have to do is edit the file, set the property to the desired number of transition buttons to display as shown (we are setting the number of transition buttons to 3), and restart Jira:

```
ops.bar.group.size.opsbar-transitions=3
```

> If you do not see the `jira-config.properties` file, you can simply create a new file with the same name and add your properties there.

See the following screenshot:

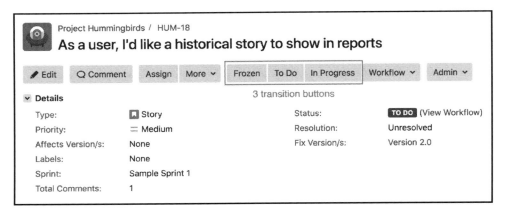

Jira now shows three transition buttons instead of two.

Restricting the resolution values in a transition

Normally, issue resolution values such as **Fixed** and **Won't Fix** are global, so regardless of the project and issue type, the same set of values will be available. As you implement different workflows in Jira, you may find that certain resolutions are not relevant for a given project or issue type.

In this recipe, we will select a subset of the global resolutions available when we close issues using our **Simple Workflow**.

How to do it...

Perform the following steps to selectively include a subset of resolutions for a given workflow transition:

1. Select and edit the **Simple Workflow**.
2. Select the **Close Issue** workflow transition.
3. Click on the **Properties** option.

4. Enter `jira.field.resolution.include` for the **Property Name** and the IDs (comma separated) for resolutions we want to make available into **Property Value**. So, if we want to only include the **Done**, **Won't Do**, and **Duplicate** resolutions, we need to specify the `10000`, `10001`, and `10002` values as the property values, with no spaces in between.

Take a look at the following screenshot:

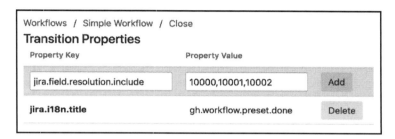

5. Click on **Publish Draft** to apply the change.

Note that the actual values for the three resolutions might be different for your Jira instance. Please double-check their values when configuring the property.

There's more...

Other than selecting a subset of resolutions, there is also a `jira.field.resolution.exclude` property that lets you exclude a subset of resolutions from the global list.

Preventing issue updates in selected statuses

By default, when an issue is in the **Closed** status, it cannot be updated. It is a good practice to make issues read-only when they are in a status that signifies logical completion.

In this recipe, we will make sure that, when an issue is moved to the **Frozen** status, it can no longer be updated until it is moved back to the **Open** status.

How to do it...

Perform the following steps to make an issue read-only when it is in the **Frozen** status:

1. Select and edit the workflow to update.
2. Select the **Frozen** workflow status.
3. Click on the **Properties** link from the panel on the right-hand side.
4. Enter `jira.issue.editable` for **Property Key** and `false` into **Property Value**, and click on **Add**.
5. Click on **Publish Draft** to apply the change.

Making a field required during a workflow transition

Using field configuration to make a field required will make the field required all the time. There are many use cases where you will only need the field to be required during certain workflow transitions.

Getting ready

For this recipe, we need to have the JSU Automation Suite for Jira Workflows app installed. You can download it from the following link, or install it directly using the UPM: `https://marketplace.atlassian.com/plugins/com.googlecode.jira-suite-utilities`.

How to do it...

Perform the following steps to make the **Reason for Freezing** field required during the **Frozen** transition:

1. Select and edit the **Simple Workflow**.
2. Select **Diagram** mode.
3. Click on the **Frozen** global workflow transition.
4. Click on the **Validators** link from the panel on the right-hand side.
5. Click on **Add validator**, select **Fields Required (JSU)** from the list, and click on **Add**.

6. Select the **Reason for Freezing** field from **Available fields** and click on **Add >>**. This will add the selected field to the **Required fields** list, as seen in the next screenshot:

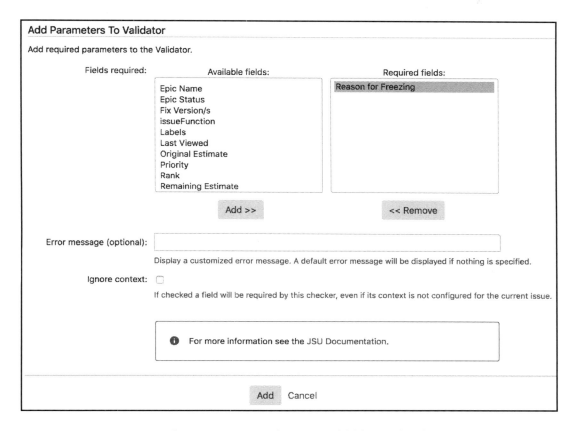

7. Enter an optional error message if you would like to display a customized message instead of the default error message.
8. Click on the **Add** button to complete the validator setup.
9. Click on **Publish Draft** to apply the change.

After you have added the validator, if you try to execute the **Frozen** transition without specifying a value for the **Reason for Freezing** field, Jira will prompt you with an error message, as shown in the following screenshot:

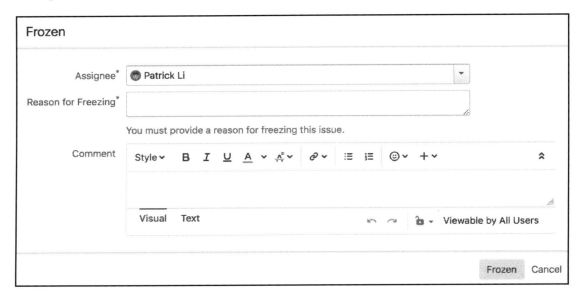

Creating custom workflow transition logic

In previous recipes, we have looked at using workflow conditions, validators, and post functions that come out of the box with Jira and from other third-party apps.

In this recipe, we will take a look at how to use scripts to define our own validation rules for a workflow validator. We will address a common use case, which is to make a field required during a workflow transition only when another field is set to a certain value.

So, our validation logic will be as follows:

- If the **Resolution** field is set to **Done**, the **Solution Details** field will be required.
- If the **Resolution** field is set to a value other than **Fixed**, the **Solution Details** field will not be required.

Getting ready

For this recipe, we need to have the ScriptRunner for Jira app installed. You can download it from the following link, or install it directly using the UPM: `https://marketplace.atlassian.com/plugins/com.onresolve.jira.groovy.groovyrunner`.

You might also want to get familiar with Groovy scripting (`http://groovy.codehaus.org`).

How to do it...

Perform the following steps to set up a validator with custom-scripted logic:

1. Select and edit the **Simple Workflow**.
2. Select **Diagram** mode.
3. Click on the **Done** global workflow transition.
4. Click on the **Validators** link from the panel on the right-hand side.
5. Click on **Add validator**, select **Script Validator** [ScriptRunner] from the list, and click on **Add**.
6. Select the **Simple scripted validator** option.
7. Enter the following script code in the **Condition** text box:

```
import com.opensymphony.workflow.InvalidInputException
import com.atlassian.jira.component.ComponentAccessor
import com.atlassian.jira.issue.CustomFieldManager
import org.apache.commons.lang3.StringUtils

def customFieldManager = ComponentAccessor.getCustomFieldManager()
def solutionField =
customFieldManager.getCustomFieldObjectByName("Solution Details")
def resolution = issue.getResolution().getName()
String solution = issue.getCustomFieldValue(solutionField)

if(resolution == "Done" && StringUtils.isBlank(solution)) {
    false
} else {
    true
}
```

8. **Enter** `You must provide the Solution Details if the Resolution is set to Done.` in the **Error** field.
9. Select **Solution Details** for **Field**.
10. Click on the **Add** button to complete the validator setup.

11. Click on **Publish Draft** to apply the change.

Your validator configuration should look something like the following screenshot:

Once we add our custom validator, the Groovy script will run every time the resolve issue transition is executed. If the **Resolution** field is set to **Done** and the **Solution Details** field is empty, we will get a message from the **Error** field, as shown in the following screenshot:

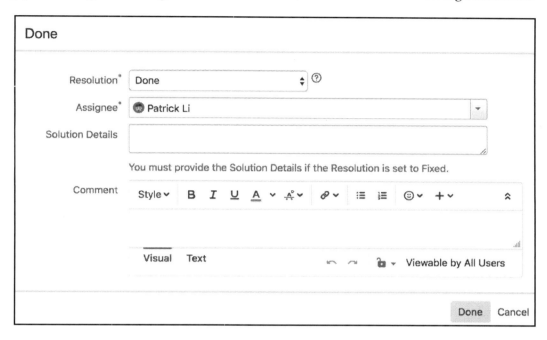

We will now see how these steps work.

How it works...

The Script Validator works just like any other validator, except that we can define our own validation logic using Groovy scripts. So, let's go through the script, and see what it does.

We first get the **Solution Details** custom field via its name, as shown in the following line of code. If you have more than one custom field with the same name, you need to use its ID instead of its name:

```
def solutionField = customFieldManager.getCustomFieldObjectByName("Solution
Details")
```

We then select the resolution value and obtain the value entered for **Solution Details** during the transition, as follows:

```
def resolution = issue.getResolutionObject().getName()
String solution = issue.getCustomFieldValue(solutionField)
```

In our example, we check the resolution name; we can also check the ID of the resolution by changing `getName()` to `getId()`.

 If you have multiple custom fields with the same name, use `getId()`.

Lastly, we check whether the **Resolution** value is **Done** and the **Solution Details** value is blank. In this case, we return a value of `false`, so the validation fails. All other cases will return the value `true`, so the validation passes. We also use `StringUtils.isBlank(solution)` to check for blank values so that we can catch cases when users enter empty spaces for the **Solution Details** field.

There's more...

You are not limited to creating scripted validators. With the ScriptRunner for Jira app, you can create scripted conditions and post functions using Groovy scripts.

4
User Management

User management is one of the most tedious, yet important, aspects of any system. It lays the foundation for many other system functions, such as security and notifications.

In this chapter, we will look at the different options available to create user accounts in Jira, and also how to manage users by using groups and project roles. We will also look at how to integrate Jira with external user-management systems, such as **Lightweight Directory Access Protocol (LDAP)**, for both authentication and user management. Lastly, we will cover how to make Jira participate in various single sign-on environments.

In this chapter, we will cover the following topics:

- Creating and importing multiple users
- Enabling public user signup
- Managing groups and group memberships
- Managing project roles
- Managing default project role memberships
- Deactivating a user
- Integrating and importing users from LDAP
- Integrating with LDAP for authentication only
- Integrating with Atlassian Crowd
- Setting up single sign-on with Crowd
- Setting up single sign-on with Google
- Setting up Windows domain single sign-on

Creating and importing multiple users

As a Jira administrator, it is usually your responsibility to set up accounts for the new user whenever someone new joins the organization. This is usually fine on an ad hoc basis, but from time to time, you might be required to import many users at once. In these cases, you will need some additional tools to help you efficiently enable all these users to access the system without any delay.

Getting ready

For this recipe, we will need the Jira **command-line interface (CLI)**. You can retrieve it from `https://marketplace.atlassian.com/plugins/org.swift.jira.cli/cloud/overview`.

The CLI app has two components. The first component is an app called CLI Connector that you can install via the **Universal Plugin Manager** (**UPM**) just like any other Jira apps. The second component is the actual CLI Client, which we will use to issue commands to Jira. You can download the latest command-line tool (`atlassian-cli-8.x.x-distribution.zip`) from `https://bobswift.atlassian.net/wiki/spaces/info/pages/103022955/Downloads+-+CLI+Clients`.

You will also need to have an administrator account, as user creation is an administrative task.

How to do it...

Before we can start using the command-line client to import users into Jira, we first need to prepare our user data. The easiest way to do this is to create a **comma-separated values** (**CSV**) file containing the following information, in the order specified. You can use a spreadsheet application such as Microsoft Excel to create it:

Username	Password	Email	Full name	Group A
tester1	xxxxx	tester1@example.com	Test User	jira-softwareusers

The following list explains each column of the CSV file:

- **Username**: The username of the user; note that usernames in Jira need to be unique.
- **Password**: The password for the new user. You can leave it blank, and let Jira automatically generate one for you.

- **Email**: The email address for the new user. Emails can be sent out to the user for him/her to reset the password once the account is created.
- **Full name**: The full name of the new user.
- **Group**: Groups to add the new user into. If you want to add the user to multiple groups, put each group into its separate column. Note that the group name you specify must already exist in Jira.

Now that you have your data file, go through the following steps to import and create the user accounts in Jira:

1. Unzip the CLI Client into a directory on your computer (for example, /opt/cli).
2. Copy the user's CSV file to a directory on your computer (for example, /tmp/users.csv).
3. Open a Command Prompt and navigate to the directory that contains the CLI Client—that is, the directory that contains the jira.sh or jira.bat file.
4. Make sure that the jira.shfile (Linux) or jira.bat (Windows) file is executable.
5. Run the following command to import users; make sure you substitute the administrator username and password in your Jira URL:

```
./jira.sh --action addUserWithFile --server
http://localhost:8080 --password <password>
--user <username> --file /tmp/users.csv
```

 The preceding command assumes you are using Linux. If you are using Windows, use jira.bat instead.

If everything runs fine, you will see an output similar to the following one on your console:

```
User: tester1 added with password: xxxxx.  Full name is: Tester One.  Email is: tester1@example.com.
User: tester2 added with password: yyyyy.  Full name is: Tester Two.  Email is: tester2@example.com.
User: tester3 added with password: zzzzz.  Full name is: Tester Three.  Email is: tester3@example.com.
User: tester4 added with password: 9vwybjvmlbjs.  Full name is: Tester Four.  Email is: tester4@example.com.
Successful adds: 4  errors: 0  already defined users: 0
```

The result of the command, as shown in the preceding output, will show every new user added to Jira as defined in the CSV file. Since we did not specify a password for the Tester Four user, the user is assigned an autogenerated password. The last line in the output also provides a summary of the number of users added successfully and the number of failed ones, if any.

How it works...

The command-line client that we used to run the `addUserWithFile` command uses Jira's remote APIs to interact with Jira. Jira exposes many of its core functionalities via these APIs, such as the ability to create new users and issues.

When we run the `addUserWithFile` command, we pass in the CSV file that contains our new users, formatted in a way that the command-line client is able to understand and make an API call to Jira to create those users for us.

However, take note that the same security rules apply when using these remote APIs (with or without the command-line client). So in our case, since creating new users is an administrative task, we need to provide an administrator account in the command.

The Jira CLI app can do a lot more than just create users. Simply run `jira.sh` or `jira.bat` to see a full list of the commands and features it supports. The CLI Connector app installed in Jira provides many more additional remote APIs that will be used by some of the functions in the command-line client.

Enabling public user signup

In the previous recipe, we looked at how to manually create new user accounts and import users from a CSV file. These are the two options that the Jira administrators have when your Jira instance is used internally.

However, if your Jira is set up to be used by the public, such as in a support system, you would want to let your customers freely sign up for a new account, rather than having them wait for the administrator to manually create each account.

How to do it...

Go through the following steps to enable public user signup:

1. Navigate to **Administration** > **System** > **General configuration**.
2. Click on the **Edit Settings** button.
3. Set the **Mode** option to **Public** and click on **Update**.

How it works...

Jira can operate in two modes, public and private. In private mode, only the administrator can create new user accounts. For example, you can use the private mode for Jira instances that are used by internal engineering teams to track their projects.

Public mode allows anyone to sign up for new accounts. The new accounts that are created will have normal user permissions, so they will be able to start using Jira immediately:

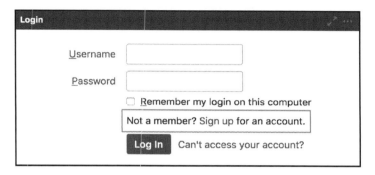

As shown in the preceding screenshot, you can sign up for a new account.

There's more...

To help prevent spammers, Jira comes with the CAPTCHA challenge response feature to make sure there is a real person signing up for a new account and not an automated bot. To enable the CAPTCHA feature, go through the following steps:

1. Navigate to **Administration** > **System** > **General configuration**.
2. Click on the **Edit Settings** button.
3. Set the **CAPTCHA on signup** option to **On**, and click on **Update**.

Once you have enabled CAPTCHA, the sign-up form will include a string of randomly generated alphanumeric characters that must be typed in correctly for a new account to be generated, as shown in the following screenshot:

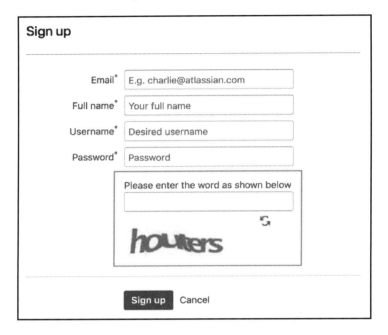

An example of CAPTCHA is shown in the preceding screenshot.

Managing groups and group memberships

In any information system, a common way of managing users is through the use of groups. Groups are based on positions and responsibilities within an organization; however, it is important to note that groups simply represent a collection of users. In Jira, groups provide an effective way to apply configuration settings, such as permissions and notifications, to users.

Groups are global in Jira—if you belong to the `jira-administrators` group, you will always be in that group regardless of the project you are accessing.

In this recipe, we will look at how to create a new group and add users to it.

How to do it...

Go through the following steps to create a new group:

1. Navigate to **Administration** > **User management** > **Groups**.
2. Enter the new group's name under the **Add group** section.
3. Click on the **Add group** button.

Go through the following steps to add users to a group:

1. Navigate to **Administration** > **User management** > **Groups**.
2. Click on the **Edit members** link for the group you want to manage.
3. Type in the usernames for the users you want to add to the group. You can click on the select user icon and use the user picker to find your users.
4. Click on the **Add selected users** button to add users to the group, as shown in the following screenshot:

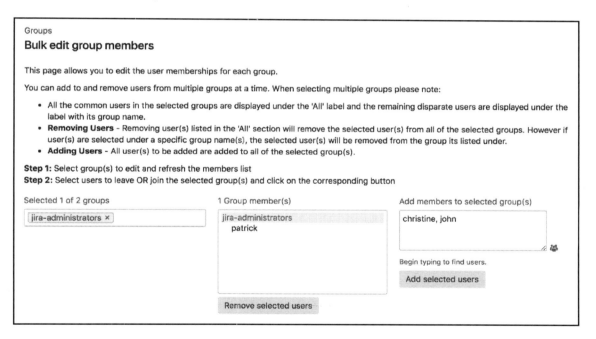

This allows you to manage users in your group.

There's more...

By editing the group's membership directly, you can add and remove multiple users to and from a group in one go; however, sometimes you only need to update a single user's group membership; in these cases, you might find it easier to manage this edit option via the user's group membership interface. Go through the following steps to edit user groups:

1. Navigate to **Administration** > **User management** > **Users**.
2. Select the **Edit user groups** option from the menu for the user you want to manage.
3. Enter the name of the group you want to add the user to. Jira provides a type-ahead feature to help you find the group you want.
4. Click on the **Join selected groups** button to add users to the group, as shown in the following screenshot:

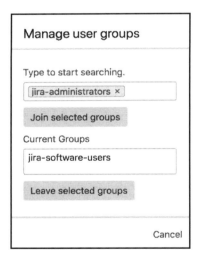

Now we have added our users to a group.

Managing project roles

Using groups is the default method of managing multiple users in Jira; however, there are some limitations with using groups. The first limitation is that groups are global in Jira. This means that if a user is in a group, then that user is included in all projects in that group.

In real life, this is often not the case—for example, suppose a user is a manager in a project. He/she may not be a manager in a different project. This becomes a problem when it comes to configuring permissions and notifications.

The second limitation is that group memberships are controlled by the Jira administrator or central IT administrator if using LDAP. This means that using groups alone to control access to the project means that it is not managed by the project owners, and can result in a bottleneck.

So, to address these limitations, Jira provides us with project roles. Project roles are similar to groups; the only difference is that the membership of a project role is defined at the project level.

How to do it...

Jira comes with three project roles out of the box—**Administrator**, **Developer**, and **User**. We will first look at how to create a new project role.

Go through the following steps to create a new project role:

1. Navigate to **Administration** > **System** > **Project roles**.
2. Enter the new project role's name and description.
3. Click on the **Add Project Role** button:

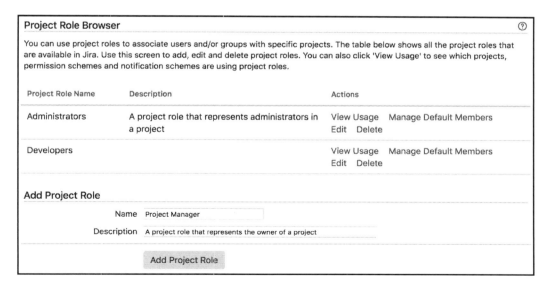

Just like groups, project roles themselves are global in Jira, but their memberships are local to each project.

Once the project role has been created, we can start adding users and groups to the relevant role for each project. To add a new user and/or group to a project role, go through the following steps:

1. Navigate to the target project.
2. Click on the **Administration** tab and select **Users and roles**.
3. Click the **Add users to a role** button.
4. Select the user and/or group, select the project role, and click on **Add**, as shown in the following screenshot:

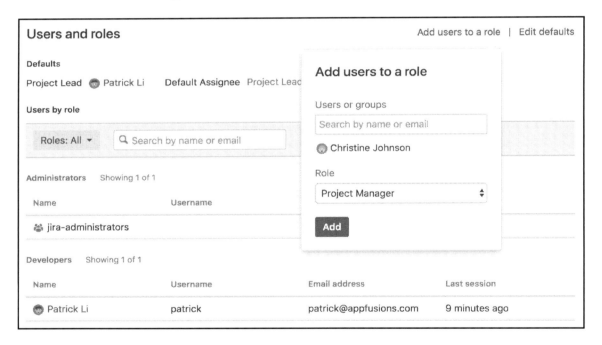

This will help you manage your project roles.

Managing default project role memberships

Project role memberships are defined per project; however, there are cases where certain users or groups need to be members of a given project role by default. In fact, Jira has the following default members out of the box:

- **Administrators**: All members of the `jira-administrators` group
- **Developers**: All members of the `jira-developers` group

With these default members, users are automatically added to the project role when a new project is created; this greatly reduces the amount of manual work required from a Jira administrator.

How to do it...

Go through the following steps to define the default membership for project roles:

1. Navigate to **Administration** > **System** > **Project roles**.
2. Click on the **Manage Default Members** link for the project role you want to configure.
3. Click on the **Edit** link of the **Default Users** column to add users to the project role.
4. Click on the **Edit** link of the **Default Groups** column to add groups to the project role, as shown in the following screenshot:

Edit Default Members for Project Role: Project Manager ⑦

The table below shows the default members (i.e. users, groups) for a project role.

NOTE: When a new project is created, it will be assigned these 'default members' for the 'Project Manager' project role. Note that 'default members' apply only when a project is created. Changing the 'default members' for a project role will not affect role membership for existing projects.
- **Return to Project Role Browser**

Default Users	Default Groups
Christine Johnson Edit	project-owners Edit

This screenshot shows how to add groups to the project role.

How it works...

Once you have assigned users and groups as the default members of a project role, any newly created project will have those users and groups added to the role. A good practice is to use groups for the default project role membership, as a user's role and responsibilities are likely to change over time.

It is important to note that changes to the default membership will *not* be retroactively applied to existing projects.

Deactivating a user

Once a user has created an issue or comment, Jira will not allow you to delete the user. In fact, deactivating a user is usually a better approach than deleting the user completely. Once the user is deactivated, the user cannot log in to Jira, and this will not count toward your license count.

 You cannot deactivate a user when you are using external user-management systems, such as LDAP or Crowd from Jira—you need to do so from the user-management system of the source.

How to do it...

Go through the following steps to deactivate a user:

1. Navigate to **Administration** > **User management** > **Users**.
2. Click on the **Edit** link for the user that is to be deactivated.
3. Uncheck the **Active** option.
4. Click on the **Update** button to deactivate the user.

Deactivated users will not be able to log in to Jira, and will have the **Inactive** option displayed next to their name.

Integrating and importing users from LDAP

By default, Jira manages its users and groups internally. Most organizations today often use LDAP, such as Microsoft **Active Directory (AD)**, for centralized user management, and you can integrate Jira with LDAP. Jira supports many different types of LDAP, including AD (https://docs.microsoft.com/en-us/windows-server/identity/ad-ds/get-started/virtual-dc/active-directory-domain-services-overview), OpenLDAP (https://www.openldap.org), and more.

There are two options for integrating Jira with LDAP. In this recipe, we will explore the first option by using an **LDAP connector**, which will periodically synchronize users, their details, and group memberships between Jira and LDAP. We will look at the second option in the next recipe, *Integrating with LDAP for authentication only*.

Getting ready

For this recipe, you will need to have an LDAP server up and running. You need to make sure that the Jira server is able to access the LDAP server and that there are no network or access issues. For example, you need to make sure that LDAP connectivity is not blocked by firewalls. At a minimum, you will also need to have the following information:

- The hostname and port number of the LDAP server.
- The base **Distinguished Name (DN)** to search for users and groups.
- The credentials to access the LDAP server. If you want Jira to be able to make changes to LDAP, make sure that the credentials have write permissions.

How to do it...

Go through the following steps to integrate Jira with an LDAP server:

1. Navigate to **Administration** > **User management** > **User Directories**.
2. Click on the **Add Directory** button and select either **Microsoft Active Directory** or **LDAP** for non-AD directories.
3. Enter the LDAP server, schema, and permission settings. Refer to the following table for more details.
4. Click on the **Quick Test** button to validate Jira's connectivity to LDAP.
5. Click on the **Save and Test** button if there are no issues with connecting to LDAP.

6. Type in a username and password to run a quick test. While doing this, make sure that Jira is able to connect to LDAP, to find the user and retrieve the user's group information, and to authenticate against LDAP.

The following tables list all the configuration parameters for configuring LDAP. Each table includes the parameters for each section on the configuration page. Let's have a look at the following table:

Server settings	Description
Name	This is an identifier for the LDAP server.
Directory Type	This selects the type of the LDAP server—for example, Microsoft Active Directory. Jira automatically fills in the user and group schema details based on the type selected.
Hostname	This is the host of the LDAP server is hosted.
Port	This is the port that the LDAP server listens to for incoming connections.
Use SSL	This checks whether SSL is being used on LDAP.
Username	This is the user account that Jira uses to access LDAP. This should be a dedicated account for Jira.
Password	This is the password for the account.

The following table lists LDAP schema parameters and their descriptions:

LDAP schema	Description
Base DN	This is the root node where Jira starts the search for users and groups.
Additional User DN	This is the additional DN to further restrict a user search.
Additional Group DN	This is the additional DN to further restrict a group search.

The following table lists LDAP permissions and their descriptions:

LDAP permission	Description
Read Only	Select this option if you do not want Jira to make any changes to LDAP. This is the ideal option if everything, including the user's group memberships, is managed with LDAP.
Read Only, with Local Groups	This option is similar to the **Read Only** option but lets you manage group memberships locally within Jira. With this option, the group membership changes you make will remain in Jira only. This is the ideal option when you only need user information from LDAP and want to manage Jira-related groups locally.
Read/Write	Select this option if you want Jira to be able to make direct changes to LDAP, assuming that Jira's LDAP account has the write permission as well.

The following screenshot shows how to test the settings:

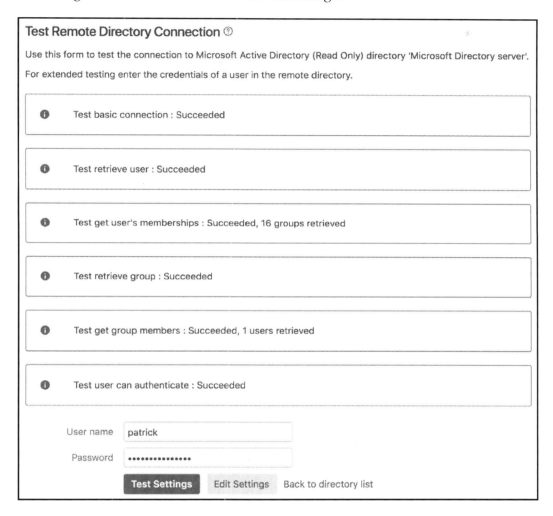

After you have added your LDAP server as a user directory, Jira will automatically start synchronizing its user and group data. Depending on the size of your LDAP, it may take a few minutes to complete the initial synchronization. You can click on **Back to directory list** to go to the directory list link and see the status of the synchronization process.

Once the process is completed, you will be able to see all your LDAP users and groups and use your LDAP credentials to access Jira.

How it works...

What we have just created in this recipe is called a connector. With a connector, Jira first pulls user and group information from LDAP and then creates a local copy. It then periodically synchronizes any deltas.

All authentication will be delegated to LDAP. So, if a user's password is updated in LDAP, it will be immediately reflected when the user attempts to log in to Jira. It is important to note that, with LDAP, users must still be in the necessary groups (for example, `jira-users`, by default) in order to access Jira, so you need to make sure that you either create a group called `jira-users` in LDAP and add everyone to it or grant the application access to LDAP groups, such as a group called `all-employees`.

Also, note that only users who have access to Jira will count toward your license count. This includes users in groups that have been granted application access to Jira.

See also

If you have a large user base in LDAP, and you only want to use LDAP for authentication, you may want to refer to the next recipe, *Integrating with LDAP for authentication only*.

Integrating with LDAP for authentication only

Sometimes, you might need LDAP only for authentication, and want to keep the group membership separate from LDAP for easy management. In this recipe, we will look at how to integrate Jira with LDAP only for authentication.

Getting ready

For this recipe, you will need to have an LDAP server up and running. You need to make sure that the Jira server is able to access the LDAP server. For more details, refer to the previous recipe, *Integrating and importing users from LDAP*.

How to do it...

Go through the following steps to integrate Jira with an LDAP server exclusively for authentication:

1. Navigate to **Administration** > **User management** > **User Directories**.
2. Click on the **Add Directory** button and select the **Internal with LDAP Authentication** option.
3. Enter the LDAP server and schema settings. Most of the parameters are identical to those you use when creating a normal LDAP connection, with a few exceptions. Refer to the following table for details.
4. Click on the **Quick Test** button to validate Jira connectivity to LDAP.
5. Click on the **Save and Test** button if there are no issues connecting to LDAP.

The following table lists configuration parameters that are specific for the **Internal with LDAP Authentication** option:

Server settings	Description
Copy User on Login	This automatically copies the user from LDAP into Jira when the user first successfully logs in to Jira.
Default Group Membership	This automatically adds the user into the groups specified here when the user first successfully logs in to Jira. This setting is not retrospectively applied to existing users. This is a useful feature to ensure that every user who can log in to Jira will be added to the necessary groups, such as `jira-users`.
Synchronize Group Memberships	This automatically copies the user's group membership to Jira when the user successfully logs in.

How it works...

This authentication option is similar to the previous recipe, but with a number of key differences:

- LDAP is only used for authentication
- Jira does not periodically synchronize the user and group information from LDAP after the initial user login
- Jira has read-only access to LDAP
- Group membership is managed inside Jira

With this setup, every time a user first successfully logs in to Jira, the user is copied from LDAP to Jira's local user repository, along with the group membership (if configured to do so). Since LDAP is only used at authentication time, with no initial overhead of synchronizing all the user information, this option can provide better performance for organizations that need to synchronize a large user base in LDAP.

Integrating with Atlassian Crowd

In the previous recipe, *Integrating with LDAP for authentication only*, we looked at how to integrate Jira with an LDAP server for user and group information. Besides using LDAP, another popular option is to use **Crowd**, which is available at `https://www.atlassian.com/software/crowd/overview`.

Crowd is a user-identity-management solution from Atlassian, and Jira supports Crowd integration out of the box. With Crowd, you can also set up a single sign-on option with other Crowd-enabled applications.

Getting ready

For this recipe, you will need to have a Crowd server up and running. You need to make sure that the Jira server is able to access the Crowd server without any glitches—for example, you need to make sure that it is not blocked by firewalls.

At a minimum, you will also need to have the following information:

- The Crowd server URL
- Credentials for the registered application in Crowd for Jira

How to do it...

Go through the following steps to integrate Jira with Crowd for user management:

1. Navigate to **Administration** > **User management** > **User Directories**.
2. Click on the **Add Directory** button and select the Atlassian Crowd option.
3. Enter the Crowd server settings. Refer to the following table for details.
4. Click on the **Test Settings** button to validate Jira's connectivity with Crowd.
5. Click on the **Save and Test** button if there are no issues connecting with Crowd.

The following tables list configuration parameters for setting up integration with Crowd:

Server settings	Description
Name	This is an identifier for the Crowd server.
Server URL	This is the Crowd's server URL.
Application Name	This is the registered application name for Jira inside Crowd.
Application Password	This is the password for the registered application.
Crowd Permissions	This is the column header.
Read Only	Select this option if you do not want Jira to make any changes to Crowd. This is the ideal option if everything, including the user's group membership, is managed with Crowd.
Read/Write	Select this option to let Jira synchronize any changes back to Crowd.

The advanced settings are listed in the following table:

Advanced settings	Description
Enable Nested Groups	This allows groups to contain other groups as members.
Enable Incremental Synchronization	This will only synchronize deltas. Enabling this option can help improve performance.
Synchronization Interval	This determines how often (in minutes) Jira should synchronize with Crowd for changes. Shorter intervals may cause performance issues.

See also

Refer to the *Setting up a single sign-on with Crowd* recipe to learn how to take advantage of Crowd's single sign-on capability with Jira and other Crowd-enabled applications.

Setting up a single sign-on functionality with Crowd

In previous recipes, we have looked at the different options available for Jira to use external centralized user repositories, including Crowd. One of the advantages of integrating Jira with Crowd is its **single sign-on (SSO)** abilities.

Web-based applications integrated with Crowd are able to participate in an SSO environment, so when a user is logged in to one application, he/she will be automatically logged in to all other applications.

If you are looking for single sign-on functionalities in a Windows environment, where users will be automatically logged on to applications with their workstation, read the next recipe, *Setting up a Windows domain single sign-on*.

Getting ready

Before you can set up SSO with Crowd, you first need to integrate Jira with Crowd for user management. Refer to the *Integrating with Atlassian Crowd* recipe for details.

If you have already integrated Jira with Crowd, you will need to have the following information:

- The application name assigned to Jira in Crowd
- The password for Jira to access Crowd
- A copy of the `crowd.properties` file from the `CROWD_INSTALL/client/conf` directory

How to do it...

Go through the following steps to enable SSO with Crowd:

1. Shut down Jira if it is running.
2. Open the `seraph-config.xml` file located in the `JIRA_INSTALL/atlassian-jira/WEB-INF/classes` directory in a text editor.
3. Locate the line that contains `com.atlassian.jira.security.login.JiraSeraphAuthenticator`. Comment it out so that it looks like the following:

   ```
   <!--
   <authenticator  class="com.atlassian.jira
   .security.login.JiraSeraphAuthenticator"/>
   -->
   ```

4. Locate the line that contains `com.atlassian.jira.security.login.SSOSeraphAuthenticator`. Uncomment it so that it looks like the following:

   ```
   <authenticator class="com.atlassian.jira
   .security.login.SSOSeraphAuthenticator"/>
   ```

5. Copy the `crowd.properties` file to the `JIRA_INSTALL/atlassian-jira/WEB-INF/classes` directory.

6. Open `crowd.properties` in a text editor and update the properties listed in the following table.

7. Start up Jira again.

The following table lists the configuration parameters from the `crowd.properties` file:

Parameter	Value
`application.name`	This is the application name configured in Crowd for Jira.
`application.password`	This is the password for the application.
`application.login.url`	This is Jira's base URL (you can get this from Jira's general configurations).
`crowd.base.url`	This is Crowd's base URL.
`session.validationinterval`	This is the duration (in minutes) that a Crowd SSO session will remain valid. Setting this to 0 will invalidate the session immediately, and will have a performance penalty. It is recommended that you set this at a higher value.

Once Jira has started up again, it will participate in SSO sessions in all Crowd SSO-enabled applications—for example, if you have multiple Jira instances integrated with Crowd for SSO, you will only need to log in to one of Jira's.

 Make sure you also have a backup copy of the file before you make any changes.

Setting up a single sign-on with Google

If your organization uses Google to manage user details, or you simply want to allow people with valid Google accounts to be able to log into your Jira instance (especially if it is a public instance), you can integrate Jira with Google so that users can log into Jira with their Google account details with a single click.

Getting ready

For this recipe, we will need the Jira CLI. You can get it at `https://docs.appfusions.com/display/GAPPSAUTHJ/Downloads+and+Notes`.

How to do it...

The first step to set up SSO with Google is to create a set of Google API credentials by going through the following steps:

1. Browse to Google API Console at `https://console.developers.google.com/apis/credentials`.
2. Click on the **Create credentials** drop-down menu.
3. Select **OAuth client ID** and then **Web application**.
4. Enter a name for the API credential and your Jira's URL for authorized JavaScript origins.
5. Create the new API credential and note down the **Client ID** and **Client Secret**: we will need them both later.

With the Google API credentials created, we can configure the SSO integration:

1. Navigate to **Administration** > **Manage apps** > **Google SSO**.
2. Click on the **Edit this configuration...** link at the bottom of the page.
3. Enter the **Client ID** and **Client Secret** from earlier.
4. Select where you would like the Google sign-in button to appear on the login page.
5. Click on **Save** to apply the changes:

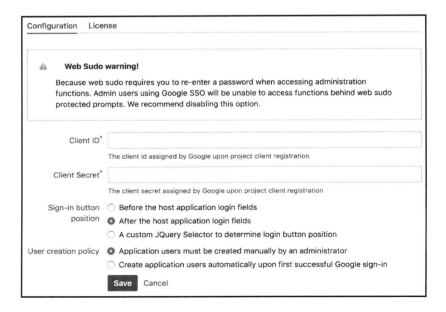

Since we will be logging into Jira via Google, it is recommended that you disable web `sudo`, as Jira does not know the Google user account's password.

Once you have configured Jira with Google API credentials, a new **Sign in with Google** button will be displayed on Jira's login page, as shown in the following screenshot:

Clicking on that will take you to Google's login page if you are not already logged into Google, or pass you straight through if you are already logged into Google. Now you are ready to log into Jira.

Setting up a Windows domain single sign-on

If your organization is running a Windows domain, you can configure Jira so that users are automatically logged in when they log in to the domain with their workstations.

Getting ready

For this recipe, we will need the Kerberos SSO Authenticator for Jira. You can get it at http://www.appfusions.com/display/KBRSCJ/Home.

You will also need to have the following set up:

- A service account in AD for Jira to use
- A **service principal name (SPN)** for Jira

How to do it...

Setting up the Windows domain SSO is not a simple task, as it involves many aspects of your network configuration. It is highly recommended that you work with the product vendor and someone who is familiar with your AD environment to ensure a smooth implementation.

Go through the following steps to set up the Windows domain SSO:

1. Shut down Jira if it is running.
2. Copy `login.conf`, `krb5.conf`, and `spnego-exclusion.properties` to the `JIRA_INSTALL/atlassian-jira/WEB-INF/classes` directory.
3. Copy `appfusions-jira-seraph-4.0.0.jar` and `appfusions-spnego-r7_3.jar` to the `JIRA_INSTALL/atlassian-jira/WEB-INF/lib` directory.
4. Open the `web.xml` file located in the `JIRA_INSTALL/atlassian-jira/WEB-INF` directory in a text editor.
5. Add the following XML snippet before the `THIS MUST BE THE LAST FILTER IN THE DEFINED CHAIN` entry. Make sure you update the values for the following parameters:
   - For `spnego.krb5.conf`, use the full path to the `spnego.krb5.conf` file.
   - For `spnego.login.conf`, use the full path to the `spnego.login.conf` file.
   - For `spnego.preauth.username`, use the username of the service account.
   - For `spnego.preauth.password`, use the password of the service account:

     ```
     <filter>
     <filter-name>SpnegoHttpFilter</filter-name>

     <filter-class>net.sourceforge.spnego
     .SpnegoHttpFilter</filter-class>

     <init-param>
     ```

```
<param-name>spnego.allow.basic</param-name>

 <param-value>true</param-value>

</init-param>

<init-param>

 <param-name>spnego.allow.localhost
 </param-name>

 <param-value>true</param-value>

</init-param>

<init-param>

 <param-name>spnego.allow.unsecure.basic
 </param-name>

 <param-value>true</param-value>

</init-param>

<init-param>

 <param-name>spnego.login.client.module
 </param-name>

 <param-value>spnego-client</param-value>

</init-param>

<init-param>

 <param-name>spnego.krb5.conf</param-name>

 <param-value>FULL_PATH/krb5.conf
 </param-value>

</init-param>

<init-param>

 <param-name>spnego.login.conf</param-name>

 <param-value>FULL_PATH/login.conf
 </param-value>
```

```xml
</init-param>

<init-param>

 <param-name>spnego.preauth.username
 </param-name>

 <param-value>SPN_USERNAME</param-value>

</init-param>

<init-param>

 <param-name>spnego.preauth.password
 </param-name>

 <param-value>SPN_PASSWORD</param-value>

</init-param>

<init-param>

 <param-name>spnego.login.server.module
 </param-name>

 <param-value>spnego-server</param-value>

</init-param>

<init-param>

 <param-name>spnego.prompt.ntlm</param-name>

 <param-value>true</param-value>

</init-param>

<init-param>

 <param-name>spnego.logger.level</param-name>

 <param-value>1</param-value>

</init-param>

<init-param>

 <param-name>spnego.skip.client.internet
```

```
</param-name>

<param-value>false</param-value>

</init-param>

</filter>
```

6. Add the following XML snippet before the `login` entry:

    ```
    <filter-mapping>
    <filter-name>SpnegoHttpFilter</filter-name>
    <url-pattern>/*</url-pattern>
    </filter-mapping>
    ```

7. Open the `seraph-config.xml` file located in the `JIRA_INSTALL/atlassian-jira/WEB-INF/classes` directory in a text editor.

8. Locate the line that contains `com.atlassian.jira.security.login.JiraSeraphAuthenticator`. Comment it out so that it looks like the following:

    ```
    <!--
    <authenticator class=
    "com.atlassian.jira.security
    .login.JiraSeraphAuthenticator"/>
    -->
    ```

9. Add the following XML snippet under the line that's been commented out:

    ```
    <authenticator
    class="com.appfusions.jira.SeraphAuthenticator"
    />
    ```

10. Restart Jira.

11. Add your Jira's URL to the local intranet zone in your browser.

 Once Jira is restarted, you should be automatically logged in every time you log into the Windows domain. Make sure you also have a backup copy of the file before making any changes.

5
Jira Security

Security is one of the most important aspects of any information system. With Jira, this includes managing different levels of access and ensuring that information is accessible only to authorized users.

In this chapter, we will cover the different levels of access control in Jira. We will also cover other security-related topics, including enforcing password strength and capturing and auditing changes in Jira for regulatory compliance.

In this chapter, we will cover the following recipes:

- Granting access to Jira
- Granting Jira System Administrator access
- Controlling access to a project
- Controlling access to Jira issue operations
- Allowing users to control permissions
- Delegating administrator permissions
- Restricting access to projects based on reporter permissions
- Setting up password policies
- Capturing electronic signatures for changes
- Changing the duration of the 'remember me' cookies
- Changing the default session timeout

Granting access to Jira

Since Jira is now a platform that includes Jira Core, Jira Software, Jira Service Desk, and other third-party applications, you can have multiple applications running on the same platform instance. This is because user access is granted on a per-application level. In this recipe, we will look at managing access to applications in Jira.

How to do it...

To grant Jira access to a group, perform the following steps:

1. Log in to Jira as a Jira Administrator.
2. Navigate to **Administration** > **Applications** > **Application access**.
3. Select and add the group to gain access to the application:

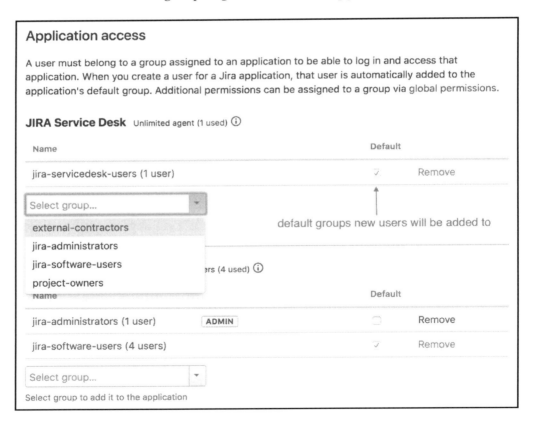

It's time to look at how the steps work.

How it works...

Starting with JIRA 7, Atlassian introduced the new concept of **applications**. This turns Jira into a platform, and major features, such as JIRA Agile (now called Jira Software) and Jira Service Desk, are now separate applications that run on the Jira platform. These changes mean that you can now control user access to each of the applications individually. Instead of using permissions to control who can access Jira, you can assign access rights based on the application.

When it comes to granting access to applications, you can only do that through groups. So, you need to ensure that you have designed your groups appropriately in order for users to have access to the correct applications.

 If you are in a group with Jira Administrators global permission (refer to the next recipe), such as `jira-administrators`, but the group does not have access to the Jira Software application, then you will still be able to log in to Jira and perform administrative tasks, but you will not have access to any projects and issues.

There's more...

If you have assigned more than one group to an application from the application access page, you can select one or more groups as the default group. This means that, when new users are added to the system, they will be automatically added to the default group, so they can start using Jira right away.

Granting Jira System Administrator access

In the previous recipe, we demonstrated how to grant access to applications in Jira to users. In this recipe, we will take a look at how to grant administrative access to users. In the same way as granting user access, you can only grant administrative access to a group of users.

How to do it...

To grant administrative access to a group in Jira, perform the following steps:

1. Navigate to **Administration** > **System** > **Global permissions**.
2. Select the **Jira System Administrators** option from the **Permissions** list, and select the group you want to grant access to, as shown in the following screenshot:

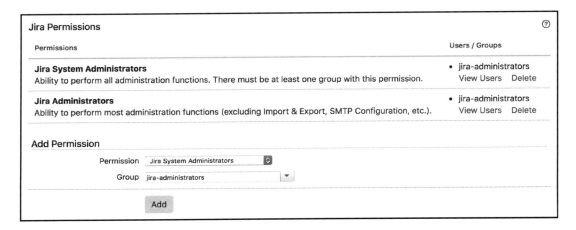

Let's understand the working now.

How it works...

There are two levels of administrative access in Jira: **Jira Administrator** and **Jira System Administrator**. For the most part, they have identical functions when it comes to Jira configurations, such as custom fields and workflows. Jira System Administrators have additional access to system-wide application configurations, such as the SMTP mail server configuration, installing apps, and updating Jira licenses.

Out of the box, the `jira-administrators` group has the global permissions of both Jira Administrator and Jira System Administrator. If you want to distinguish between the two different levels of administration, you can create two separate groups and grant them different permissions.

Controlling access to a project

In the previous recipes, we looked at how to use global permissions to control Jira access and administrator-level access. In this recipe, we will demonstrate how to control project-level permissions, starting with access to projects.

Getting ready

To control project-level access, we use permission schemes. Jira comes with a default permission scheme, which is applied automatically to all projects. You can use this scheme and update its permission settings directly. For this recipe, we will start by creating a new permission scheme to illustrate the whole process. If you want to just use the default scheme, you can skip the first three steps.

How to do it...

First, we need to create a new permission scheme, which can be done through the following steps:

1. Navigate to **Administration** > **Issues** > **Permission schemes**.
2. Click on the **Add Permission Scheme** button.
3. Enter the new scheme's name and click on **Add**.
4. With the permission scheme created, we then need to grant permissions to users and groups, namely, the **Browse Projects** permission, which controls access to projects.
5. Click on the **Permissions** link for the new permission scheme.
6. Click on the **Edit** link for the **Browse Projects** permission.

7. Select who to grant the permission to. For example, if you want to limit access to only members of a group, you can select the **Group** option, choose the target group, and click on **Grant**:

We can grant permissions to multiple users and groups, and, once finished, we can apply the permission scheme to the project that we want:

1. Go to the project that you want to apply the permission scheme to and click on the **Administration** tab.
2. Select the **Permissions** option on the left-hand side, and click on the **Use a different scheme** option from the **Actions** menu:

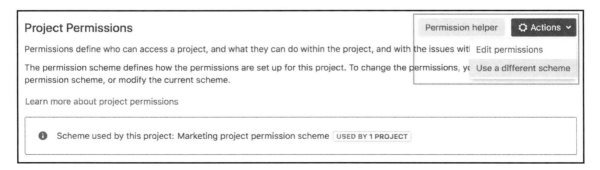

3. Select the new permission scheme and click on **Associate**.

How it works...

Permission schemes define project-level permissions. Unlike global permissions, which can only be granted to groups, these can be granted to specific users, groups, project roles, and more. The option you choose here will depend on your use case. Generally speaking, groups will be the most straightforward option, as users often belong to one or more groups and you can easily model your permission requirements based on groups. Other options are useful when you have special or edge cases where you need to accommodate users that do not fit into your group setup. Once the permission scheme is configured, you can apply the scheme to individual projects. In this way, different projects can have different permission schemes to suit their needs.

Controlling access to Jira issue operations

In this recipe, we will take a look at permissions that control issue operations. These are the operations that your end users will perform on a daily basis, including create, edit, delete, comment, and more.

Getting ready

Just as we saw in the previous recipe, you can either use an existing permission scheme or create a new permission scheme. For this recipe, we will continue working with the permission scheme that we created previously.

How to do it...

To set up permission schemes for issue operations, perform the following steps:

1. Go to the project that you want to apply the permission scheme to and click on the **Administration** tab.

2. Select the **Permissions** option on the left-hand side and click on the **Edit Permissions** option from the **Actions** menu:

3. Click on the **Edit** link for the permissions that you want to update, such as **Create Issue** and **Edit Issue**. Note that issue-related permissions are grouped under the **Issue permissions** heading.
4. Select the target to grant the permission to and click on **Grant**.

There's more...

If in doubt, or if you have users reporting permission-related issues, you can always use the **Permission helper** tool (shown in the following screenshot) to check your configurations. All you have to do is enter the user's username, select an issue that is in the project, choose the type of permission, and click on **Submit**. The tool will go through your permission configurations and display a report that explains what is required for the selected permission so that you can work out why the user does or does not have the selected permission:

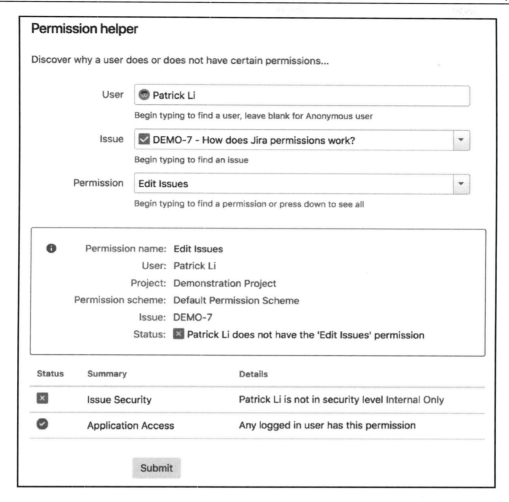

Permission helper

Discover why a user does or does not have certain permissions...

User ⬤ Patrick Li

Begin typing to find a user, leave blank for Anonymous user

Issue ☑ DEMO-7 - How does Jira permissions work? ▾

Begin typing to find an issue

Permission Edit Issues ▾

Begin typing to find a permission or press down to see all

ℹ Permission name: Edit Issues
User: Patrick Li
Project: Demonstration Project
Permission scheme: Default Permission Scheme
Issue: DEMO-7
Status: ☒ Patrick Li does not have the 'Edit Issues' permission

Status	Summary	Details
☒	Issue Security	Patrick Li is not in security level Internal Only
✓	Application Access	Any logged in user has this permission

Submit

You will always be asked to select an issue when using the **Permission helper** tool, even if you want to check a project-level permission, such as administer projects. In this case, simply select an issue that belongs to the project, and the tool will verify the permission for you.

Allowing users to control permissions

When you have a mixed group of users (such as internal employees and outside consultants) working on the same Jira project, there will be instances regarding sensitive information that should only be viewed by internal employees. In these cases, you will want to mark those instances as internal only, so that other people cannot see them.

In this recipe, we will demonstrate how to set up permissions to control access at the issue level with issue security schemes.

How to do it...

The steps for setting up issue-level permissions are as follows:

1. Since Jira does not come with any default issue security schemes, the first step is to create a new one from scratch:
    1. Navigate to **Administration > Issues > Issue security schemes**.
    2. Click on the **Add issue security scheme** link.
    3. Enter a name for the new scheme and then click on **Add**.
2. The second step is to set up the security levels that you can choose from, such as **Internal Users Only**:
    1. Click on the **Security Levels** link for our new issue security scheme.
    2. Enter the name for each security level and click on the **Add Security Level** button.

 You can also click on the **Default** link to make a security level the default choice. This will pre-select the default security level while creating new issues in projects that are using the issue security scheme.

The following screenshot shows the three existing security levels:

Edit Issue Security Levels

On this page you can create and delete the issue security levels for the "Internal and External Users" issue security scheme. Each security level can have users/groups assigned to them.

An issue can then be assigned a Security Level. This ensures only users who are assigned to this security level may view the issue.

Once you have set up some Security Levels, be sure to grant the "Set Issue Security" permission to relevant users.

- View all **Issue Security schemes**

Security Level	Users / Groups / Project Roles	Actions
Internal Users Only	• Group (jira-software-users) (Delete)	Add Default Edit Delete
Internal and External Users	• Group (jira-software-users) (Delete) • Group (external-contractors) (Delete)	Add Default Edit Delete
Reporter and Assignee Only	• Reporter (Delete) • Current assignee (Delete)	Add Default Edit Delete

Add Security Level

Add a new security level by entering a name and description below.

Name

Description

Add Security Level

3. After we have set up the security levels, the third step is to grant users access to each of the security levels that you have defined:
   1. Click on the **Add** link for the security level you want to set up the user access for.
   2. Select the permission option and click on the **Add** button.

The following screenshot displays the different options you have while granting security levels:

4. Now that we have all of the security levels set up, the last step is to apply the issue security scheme to our project:

1. Go to the project you want to apply the issue security scheme to and click on the **Administration** tab.

2. Select the **Issue Security** option on the left-hand side and click on the **Select a scheme option** from the **Actions** menu.

3. Select the new issue security scheme and click on **Next**.

4. If the project is not empty, Jira asks you to select a default security level for all of the issues. You can select the **None** option so that all issues remain as they are, or you can select a security level that is applied to all issues.

5. Click on the **Associate** button:

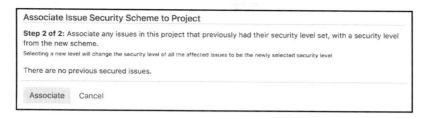

As you can see in the preceding screenshot, the issue security scheme is now applied to the project.

How it works...

The issue security scheme allows you, as an end user, to control who can access individual issues, based on the security levels set. Issues with the security level can only be viewed by those who meet the criteria. Note that the subtasks inherit security levels from their parent issues.

Once we have applied the issue security scheme to a project, users with the **Set Issue Security** permission are able to select a security level while creating and editing issues, as shown in the following screenshot:

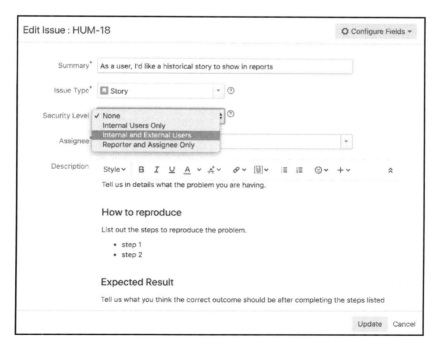

If you do not see the **Security Level** field, make sure the field is added to the screen and that you have the **Set Issue Security** permission. You can use the **Permission helper** feature covered in the previous recipe to verify this.

It is also worth mentioning that you can only select security levels that you belong to. For example, if there are two security levels, *A* and *B*, then security level *A* is granted to the jira-administrators group, and security level *B* is granted to the jira-users group. Now, as a member of the jira-users group, you will only be able to select security level *B*. This is to prevent users from accidentally locking themselves out of an issue by selecting the wrong security level.

A user who meets the criteria for the selected security level is able to view the issue normally. However, if a user who does not meet the criteria tries to view the issue, they get a permission violation error, as shown in the following screenshot:

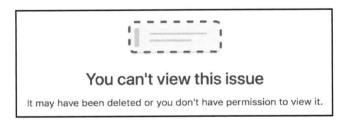

This message also informs users that the may have been deleted.

Delegating administrator permissions

Most customization and configuration options, such as workflows and screens, are managed by Jira Administrators. While this model may work well for a small organization, it often causes a bottleneck for larger organizations, where many customizations to these core Jira functions are required and there are only a few Jira Administrators who can actually make the necessary changes.

In this recipe, we will look at how you can enable project administrators to make some of these customizations themselves without having to rely entirely on Jira Administrators.

How to do it...

To allow project administrators to make customization changes, perform the following steps:

1. Navigate to **Administration** > **Issues** > **Permission schemes**.
2. Click on the **Permissions** link for the permission scheme used by the project. If there is no permission scheme specifically for the project, create a new permission scheme by first cloning the current scheme used by clicking on the **Copy** link.
3. Check the **Extended project administration** option under the **Administer Projects** permission:

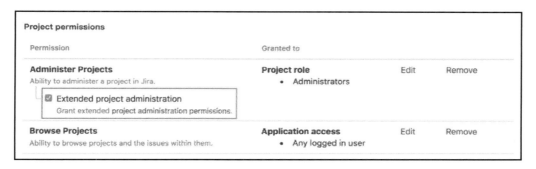

Once the permission scheme has the **Extended project administration** option enabled, administrators of projects using that permission scheme will be allowed to make changes to the project's workflows and screens.

How it works...

The **Extended project administration** option allows project administrators to make changes to workflows and screens with certain limitations:

- Workflows cannot be used by other projects.
- Only statuses that already exist in Jira can be added to workflows. Project administrators cannot create new statuses.
- The existing status in a workflow can be deleted only if no issues in the project are currently in the status.
- Workflow transitions can be deleted from the workflow, but details such as properties, validators, conditions, post-functions, and screens cannot be changed.

- Only non-system screens, that is, screens created by Jira Administrators, can be updated.
- Screens cannot be used by other projects.
- Only existing fields, both custom and system, can be added to screens.

Restricting access to projects based on reporter permissions

As you have seen in one of the previous recipes, the **Browse Projects** permission controls who can access a project in Jira. In this recipe, we will set up permissions so that users can only see projects they can create issues in and not the projects in which they cannot.

Getting ready

Since we will be making direct changes to a Jira system file, make sure you create backups for any modified files. This recipe will also require a restart of Jira, so plan this during a time slot that will not affect your users.

How to do it...

To restrict access to projects based on who can or cannot report criterion, you first need to enable a special permission type, as follows:

1. Open the `permission-types.xml` file from the `JIRA_INSTALL/atlassian-jira/WEB-INF/classes` directory in a text editor.
2. Locate the following lines, and uncomment the `reportercreate` permission type, as follows:

   ```
   <!-- Uncomment & use this permission to show only projects
   where the user has create permission and issues
   within that where they are the reporter. -->

   <!-- This permission type should only ever be assigned to
   the "Browse Projects" permission. -->

   <!-- Other permissions can use the "reporter" or "create"
   permission type as appropriate. -->
   ```

```
<!-- <type id="reportercreate" enterprise="true">
  <class>com.atlassian.jira.security.type

  .CurrentReporterHasCreatePermission</class>

</type>

-->
```

3. Restart Jira for the changes to apply.

Once the `reportercreate` permission type is enabled, a new **Reporter** option (which shows only projects with create permissions) is displayed while working with permission schemes, as shown in the following screenshot:

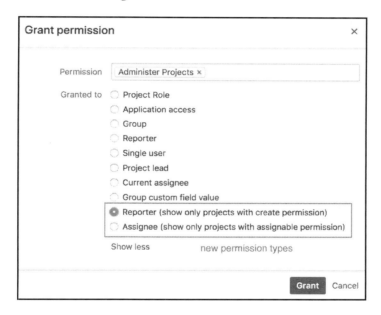

Projects with permission schemes that use this option for the **Browse Projects** permission are viewable only by users who can create issues in them.

How it works...

The `reportercreate` permission type checks whether the current user has permission to create issues in a given project. This is different than the default reporter or the current reporter permission type, which make the project visible to all users.

Additionally, note that this permission should only be applied to the **Browse Projects** permission. If applied to other permissions, especially the **Create Issues** permission, it causes Jira to go into an infinite loop, and that is the reason why this permission type is disabled by default.

There's more...

There is also a similar **Assignee** (which only shows projects with assignable permissions) permission type, which can be enabled in the permission-types.xml file. Similar to the reporter equivalent, this permission type checks whether users can be assigned issues in the project. Just like the reporter permission type, this should only be applied to the **Browse Projects** permission:

```
<!-- Uncomment & use this permission to show only projects where the user
has the assignable permission and issues within that where they are the
assignee -->

<!-- This permission type should only ever be assigned to the "Browse
Projects" permission. -->

<!-- Other permissions can use the "reporter" or "create" permission type
as appropriate. -->

<!--
<type id="assigneeassignable" enterprise="true">
  <class>com.atlassian.jira.security.type
  .CurrentAssigneeHasAssignablePermission</class>

</type>

-->
```

Setting up password policies

By default, Jira allows you to create a password of any combination and length. For security, organizations often need to have password policies such as password length and complexity to strengthen the passwords and make them difficult to guess.

In this recipe, we will demonstrate how to set up password policies in Jira to define the strength of passwords.

How to do it...

To enable and configure the password policy settings, perform the following steps:

1. Navigate to **Administration** > **System** > **Password Policy**.
2. Select from one of the predefined policy settings; alternatively, select the **Custom** option and configure the settings yourself.
3. Click on the **Update** button to enable the password policy, as shown in the following screenshot:

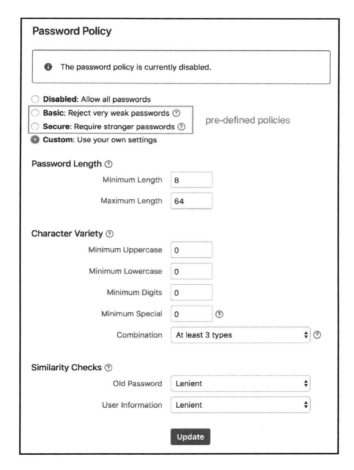

Generally, it is better to use the custom option and set your own password policy rather than using one of the predefined options, as it gives you more control and allows you to enforce more secure passwords for your users.

How it works...

With the password policy configured, every time someone tries to create a new password, Jira will make sure that the new password satisfies the policy rules. If it does not, error messages are displayed with information on the requirements, as shown in the following screenshot:

The error messages show that some rules are not satisfied.

There's more...

Apart from the built-in password policy feature, there is also a third-party app called **Enterprise Password Policy for Jira**, which provides features such as password age and user account locking to make your Jira compliant with ISO/IEC 27002. You can get the app at https://marketplace.atlassian.com/plugins/com.intenso.jira.plugins. password-policy.

After you have installed the app in Jira, there will be a new **Password Policy** section in **Manage apps**, under **Administration**. Click on the **Configure** option and then on **Password Complexity**, and you will be able to set your password policy, as shown in the following screenshot:

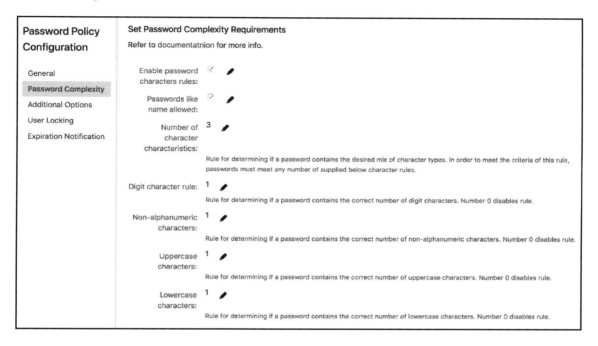

 You need to disable the default password policy feature to use this app.

As you can see from the preceding screenshot, there are more options and controls for you to define your password policies compared to the out-of-the-box feature from Jira.

Capturing electronic signatures for changes

Organizations that have strict regulatory requirements often need to capture **electronic signatures** (or **e-signatures**) as issues move along the workflow, for future auditing purposes. This is often a part of the CFR Part 11 compliance.

In this recipe, we will look at how to enforce and capture e-signatures when someone tries to transition an issue through the workflow.

Getting ready

For this recipe, we need to install the CFR Part 11 E-Signatures app. You can download the app at `https://docs.appfusions.com/display/PRT11J/Home`, and then install it in **Manage apps** in the administration console.

How to do it...

To start capturing electronic signatures, we first need to create an **Electronic Signature** custom field:

1. Navigate to **Administration** > **Issues** > **Custom fields**.
2. Click on the **Add Custom Field** button and select the **Advanced** tab.
3. Choose the **Electronic Signature** custom field type and click on **Next**.
4. Name the custom field `E-Signatures` and click on **Next**.
5. Select a screen to place the custom field onto. For example, if you want to capture signatures when users resolve an issue, you will need to select the screen used for the **Resolve Issue** transition.
6. Click on the **Update** button:

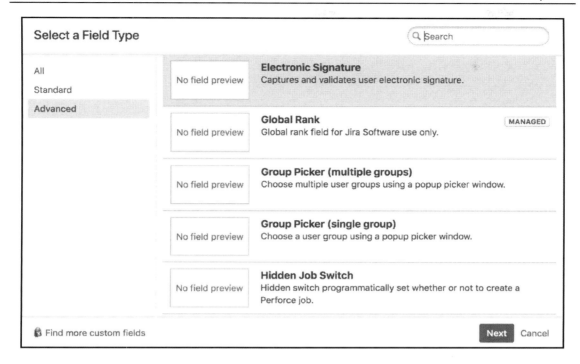

 You need to have a screen for the operations for which you want to capture electronic signatures.

How it works...

Once you have created an **Electronic Signature** custom field and added it onto a screen, such as the **Resolve Issue** screen, it will be displayed as two text fields: one for the username and one for the password.

The workflow transition can only be completed when the user signs the action by putting in their username and password, as shown in the following screenshot:

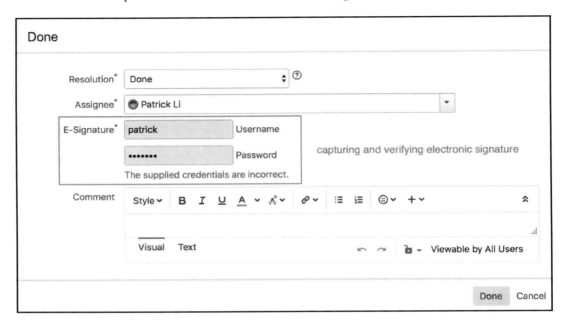

If the signature verification is successful and the transition is complete, the electronic signature will be stored, and you can get a report by clicking on the new **E-Signatures** issue tab at the bottom of the web page:

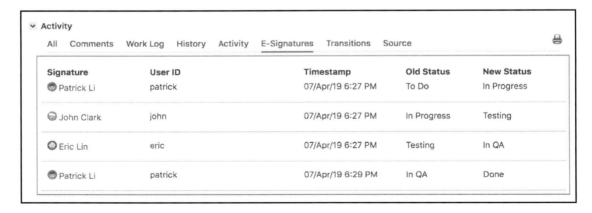

The e-signatures app also has a **Restricted Mode** option (which is turned off by default). This forces users to use their own credentials when providing e-signature. You can enable this restricted mode by performing the following steps:

1. Navigate to **Administration** > **Manage apps** > **E-Signature Fields**.
2. Check the **Restricted Mode** option and click on **Save**.

Once enabled, the username field is automatically set to the current user's username, so you can only sign with your own password.

Changing the duration of the remember me cookies

When a user selects the **Remember my login on this computer** checkbox, the user doesn't need to re-enter their credentials again from the same browser, unless they are explicitly logged out. In addition to this, by default, this feature lasts for two weeks.

In this recipe, we will look at how to change the duration, extend it to the maximum extent possible, or reduce it to be consistent with your security requirements.

Getting ready

Since we will be making direct changes to a Jira system file, make sure you create backups for any files that you modify. This recipe will also require a restart of Jira, so plan this during a time slot that will not affect your users.

How to do it...

To change the 'remember me' cookie duration, perform the following steps:

1. Open the `seraph-config.xml` file from the `JIRA_INSTALL/atlassian-jira/WEB-INF/classes` directory in a text editor.

2. Locate the `autologin.cookie.age` line, and change the value of `param-value` to the desired number in seconds:

```
<init-param>
    <param-name>autologin.cookie.age</param-name>
    <param-value>1209600</param-value>
</init-param>
```

3. Restart Jira for the changes to apply.

How it works...

Jira uses the Seraph framework (`https://docs.atlassian.com/atlassian-seraph/latest`) to manage its HTTP session cookies. When the **Remember me** option is checked, it creates `seraph.rememberme.cookie`.

The `seraph-config.xml` file is used to configure the Seraph framework and the `autologin.cookie.age` parameter is used to set the maximum age for the cookie.

See also

- You can refer to the *Changing the default session timeout* recipe for more details about how to change the default session timeout setting.

Changing the default session timeout

By default, each active user session lasts for five hours (or 300 minutes) of idle time. This means that a user can log in and leave the computer for up to five hours and their browser session will still remain active.

In this recipe, we will look at how to change the default session timeout.

Getting ready

Since we will be making direct changes to a Jira file, make sure you create backups for any files that are modified. This recipe will also require a restart of Jira, so plan this during a time slot that will not affect your users.

How to do it...

To change the session timeout settings in Jira, perform the following steps:

1. Open the `web.xml` file from the `JIRA_INSTALL/atlassian-jira/WEB-INF` directory in a text editor.

2. Locate the `<session-config>` line, and change the value of `session-timeout` to the desired number in minutes:

```
<session-config>
    <session-timeout>300</session-timeout>
</session-config>
```

3. Restart Jira for the changes to apply.

How it works...

Jira uses the standard Java session configuration in the `web.xml` file, which defines the session timeout in minutes. You can refer to this at `http://docs.oracle.com/cd/E13222_01/wls/docs81/webapp/web_xml.html#1017275`.

6
Emails and Notifications

Email is one of the most important communication tools in the world. It is a technology that people are familiar with and had the least amount of resistance in regard to its adoption. Therefore, these days email integration has become one of the key features of any system. Help-desk systems, CRMs, and even document-management systems all need to be able to both send and receive emails. So it is not surprising that Jira comes with a full list of email integration features out of the box.

In this chapter, we will learn how to configure Jira to send out email notifications every time someone makes a change to issues, set up notification rules to manage email recipients, and create mail templates to customize email content. We will also look at how Jira can process emails and create issues automatically, saving us the effort of manual data entry.

In this chapter, we will cover the following recipes:

- Setting up an outgoing mail server
- Sending emails to users from Jira
- Sending notifications for issue updates
- Sending notifications with custom templates
- Disabling outgoing notifications
- Creating mail handlers to process incoming emails
- Using emails to update Jira issues
- Setting up a project-specific From email address

Setting up an outgoing mail server

In this recipe, we will look at how to set up an outgoing mail server in Jira that can be used to send direct emails to users or automated notifications when updates are made to issues.

Getting ready

Jira requires a working mail server to send emails, and it uses the **SMTP** (short for **Simple Mail Transfer Protocol**) to communicate with the mail server. Because of this, you will need the following:

- A working mail server that is either on the same server as Jira or accessible over the network
- Connectivity details, including the mail server's host, port, protocol (SMTP or secured SMTP), and SSL certificate if it is using a self-signed certificate
- Authentication details for Jira to log in to the mail server

How to do it...

Go through the following steps to set up an outgoing mail server:

1. Log in to Jira as a Jira administrator.
2. Navigate to **Administration** > **System** > **Outgoing Mail**.
3. Click on the **Configure new SMTP mail server** button.
4. Set a name for the mail server. For example, you can use the mail server's hostname.
5. Set the **From address** field that will be used when users receive an email from Jira.
6. Provide an **Email prefix** value, which will be added to every email's subject. For example, you can use [Jira] to let users know it is coming from Jira.
7. Select whether you will be using a custom SMTP server or one from either Gmail or Yahoo! mail. If you are using Gmail or Yahoo!, make sure you select the corresponding option and provide the access credentials. If you are using a custom SMTP server, you will need to provide its hostname, port number, and credentials, if necessary.

8. Click on the **Test Connection** button, with the credentials provided, to make sure Jira is able to connect to the mail server. If the test is successful, click on the **Add** button, as shown in the following screenshot:

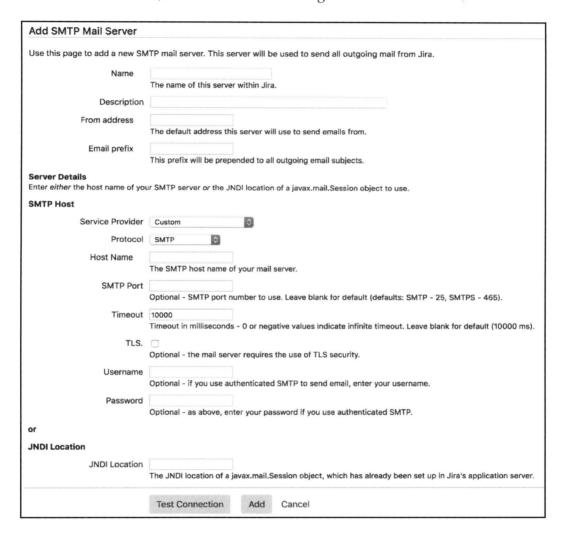

You can only have one outgoing mail server.

Once we have configured the outgoing mail server in Jira, we can send a test email to make sure everything is working properly:

1. Click on the **Send a Test Email** link.
2. Verify whether the email address in the **To** field is the one that you have access to. Jira will automatically populate it with the email address of the currently logged-in user.
3. Click on the **Send** button to send the test email.

Jira will immediately send out the test email (normal notification emails are placed in a queue before they are sent) to the address in the **To** field, with the **Subject** and **Body** content specified, as shown in the following screenshot. If there is an error, you can check the **SMTP logging** checkbox to get more details on the error:

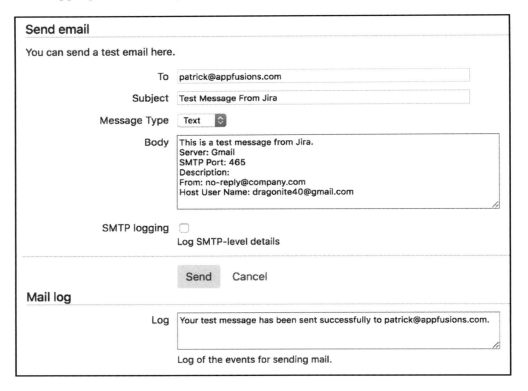

We have now successfully set up an outgoing email server.

Sending emails to users from Jira

With the outgoing mail server set up, we will now be able to send emails directly from Jira. One common use case is sending out reminders, such as system maintenance notices, to everyone in Jira, or sending important updates to members of a project. In this recipe, we will look at how to perform these types of tasks with Jira.

Getting ready

You must first configure an outgoing mail server for Jira. Refer to the previous recipe, *Setting up an outgoing mail server*, for more details.

How to do it...

Go through the following steps to send out direct emails to users in Jira:

1. Navigate to **Administration > System > Send email**.
2. Select the recipients of the email. You can choose to send an email via **Project Roles** or **Groups**. For example, to send an email to everyone who uses Jira, you can select the **jira-software-users** group (if it is the group that all of the users are in).
3. Type in your email **Subject** and **Body**.
4. Check the **Bcc** checkbox if you do not want people to see other recipients' email addresses.

5. Click on the **Send** button to send the email, as shown in the following screenshot:

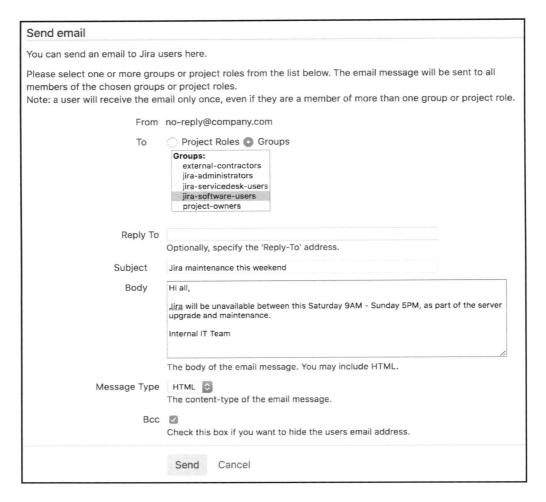

This completes the steps to send emails to users.

Sending notifications for issue updates

The other major use of outgoing mails is for Jira to automatically send out notifications about changes to issues. For example, if an issue has been updated, you would want the issue's reporter and assignee to be notified of the change.

In this recipe, we will look at how to set up notification rules so that interested parties are notified of any changes to their issues.

Getting ready

You must first configure an outgoing mail server for Jira. Refer to the *Setting up an outgoing mail server* recipe for more details.

How to do it...

Jira uses notification schemes to control who should receive notifications when there are any changes in issues. Jira comes with a default notification scheme that is applied to all projects by default. You can update this default scheme's notification settings by clicking on its **Notifications** link. In this recipe, however, we will be creating a new notification scheme and applying it to projects. If you want to use the default notification scheme, you can skip the new scheme creation steps and go straight to step 2:

1. Go through the following steps to create a new notification scheme:
    1. Navigate to **Administration** > **Issues** > **Notification schemes**.
    2. Click on the **Add notification scheme** link.
    3. Enter a name for the new scheme and click on **Add** to create it.

    After you have created a new notification scheme, you will be taken to the notification settings page for the scheme. By default, there will be no notifications set for any event.

2. To add a notification recipient to an event, go through the following steps:
    1. Click on the **Add** link for the event.
    2. Select the type of notification recipient (for example, the `Group` option, as shown in the following screenshot), and click on **Add**.

You can add a notification recipient to multiple events at the same time by using the multi-select events field. The following screenshot of the **Add Notification** page shows this:

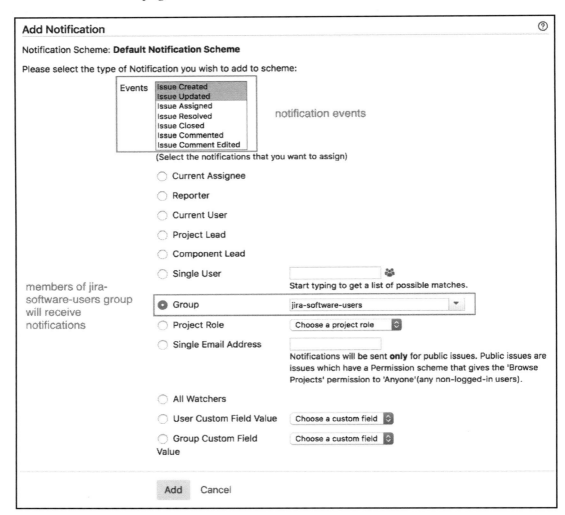

You can add as many notification recipients as you need for an event, and Jira will not send duplicate emails to the same user. For example, if you have set both the reporter and assignee to receive notifications for a single event, and they happen to be the same user, Jira will only send out one email instead of two. Also, note that Jira will take permissions into consideration when sending out notifications. If a user does not have access to the issue, Jira will not send notifications to that user.

3. The last step is to apply our new notification scheme to a project:
    1. Browse to the project you want to apply the notification scheme to.
    2. Click on the **Project settings** option.
    3. Select the **Notifications** option from the panel on the left-hand side.
    4. Select **Use a different scheme** from the **Actions** menu.
    5. Select the new notification scheme and click on **Associate**.

How it works...

Jira uses an event system where every issue operation, such as creating a new issue or workflow transition, will trigger a corresponding event to be fired. As we have seen, notification schemes map events to notification recipients. This way, we are able to set up flexible notification rules to notify different people for different events.

Jira provides many different notification recipient types. Some, such as Current Assignee and Reporter, are very simple—they will simply take the value of the current issue's assignee and reporter field respectively. Other options, such as **User Custom Field Value**, can be very flexible. For example, you can create a multi-user picker custom field, and for each issue, you can have a different list of users as recipients, without having to modify the actual scheme itself.

Events are also mapped to email templates so that Jira knows what to use for the subject and body. You cannot change the mapping for system events, but as we will see in the next recipe, we can create custom events and select which templates to use.

There's more...

Being automatically notified of any changes that happen in Jira is convenient, but if you have a busy Jira, you might find yourself buried in emails as a result of too many updates. To help with that, you can enable the new email batching feature. By enabling batching, instead of receiving an email for each update that happens to an issue, Jira will group all updates for a given issue and send you a summary email instead. To enable email batching, go through the following steps:

1. Navigate to **Administration** > **System** > **Batching email notification**.
2. Check the **Batching email notification** option to enable the feature.

Sending notifications with custom templates

In the previous recipe, *Sending notifications for issue updates*, we looked at how to set up notification schemes by mapping events to notification recipients.

In this recipe, we will expand on that and look at how to create custom events and templates to use for notifications. This has two advantages:

* We can customize the content and the look and feel of the notification email
* We can specify exactly which event will be fired for each workflow transition and set up notification rules accordingly

We will create a new event that will represent a request that has been approved by the management to proceed. This event will be triggered in an approve workflow transition and will have a custom template applied to it.

How to do it...

The first step is to create our custom email templates. All mail templates are stored in the `JIRA_INSTALL/atlassian-jira/WEB-INF/classes/templates/email` directory, and generally, for each event in Jira, there are three template files:

* **The subject template**: This is the template file for the email's subject line, which is stored in the `subject` subdirectory.

- **The text template**: This is the template file for emails sent in text format, which is stored in the `text` subdirectory.
- **The HTML template**: This is the template file for emails sent in HTML format, which is stored in the `html` subdirectory.

To start creating our own email templates, we first need to create the three files mentioned in the previous list of template files and place them in their respective directories. Take special note that all three files need to have the same filename with a `.vm` extension.

We will start with the subject template, as follows:

1. Create a new file called `issueapproved.vm` in the `subject` subdirectory with the following code snippet:

   ```
   #disable_html_escaping()

   $eventTypeName - ($issue.key) $issue.summary
   ```

2. We now need to create the body of the email, keeping in mind that we have to create two versions—one for text and one for HTML. The following snippet shows the HTML version; for the text version, simply remove the HTML markups. Note that both HTML and text template files need to be the same—that is, `issueapproved.vm`:

   ```
   #disable_html_escaping()

   Hello $issue.reporterUser.displayName,

   <p>
    Your request <a href="">$issue.key</a> has been approved, with the
   comment below:
   </p>

   <blockquote>
     <p>
      #if($comment.body)
         $comment.body
       #else
      <i>No comment</i>
       #end
     </p>
   </blockquote>

   <br/>

   Internal IT team
   ```

3. After we have created all three template files, we need to register them in Jira so that they can be selected while creating custom events. To register new email templates, open the `email-template-id-mappings.xml` file in a text editor; you can find the file inside the `JIRA_INSTALL/atlassian-jira/WEB-INF/classes` directory.

4. The `email-template-id-mappings.xml` file lists all the email templates in Jira, so we need to add a new entry at the end, as follows:

```
<templatemapping id="10002">

<name>Issue Approved</name>

<template>issueapproved.vm</template>

<templatetype>issueevent</templatetype>

</templatemapping>
```

There are a few points to note here:

- The `id` value of `<templatemapping>` needs to be unique.
- You can give any value to the `<name>` element and it will be displayed in Jira. It is good practice to keep it consistent with standard Jira event convention.
- The `<template>` element should be the name of the custom template files we have created. All three files need to have the same filename since we can only have one `<template>` element.
- The `<templatetype>` element needs to have the value set to `issueevent`.

Once you have added the entry and saved the file, you will need to restart Jira for the changes to be applied.

Now that we have our custom email templates in place, we can create the custom event that will use our new templates. Go through the following steps to create a custom event in Jira:

1. Navigate to **Administration** > **System** > **Events**.
2. Enter `Issue Approved` for the new event's name.

3. Select the **Issue Approved** template we just created.

4. Click on the **Add** button to create the new event:

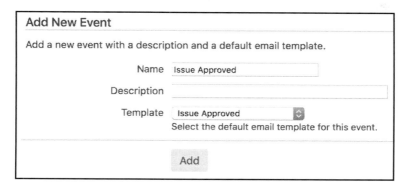

Once you have created the event, it will be available in the notification schemes, and we will be able to select who will receive email notifications by configuring our notification schemes—as shown in the following screenshot. Whenever an issue is approved, both the reporter and the user Christine will be notified:

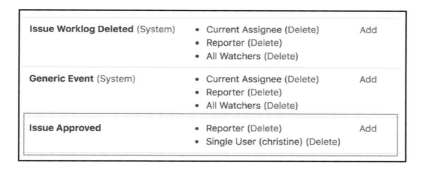

The last step is to make sure that our custom events are fired when users trigger the action:

1. Navigate to **Administration > Issues > Workflows**.

2. Click on the **Edit** link for the workflow, which contains the transitions that will fire the custom event. In this case, we will be using a simple approval workflow that contains a transition called **Approve**:

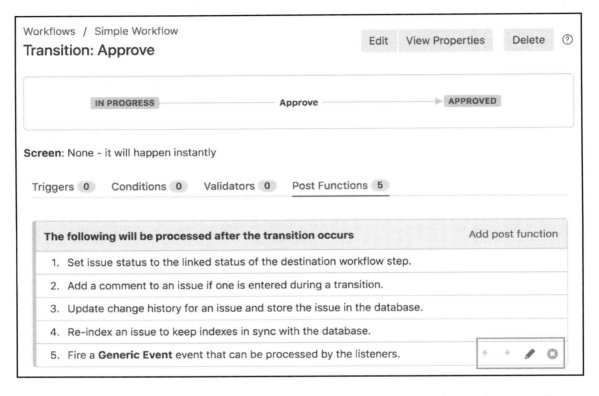

3. Click on the workflow transition, and select the **Post Functions** tab. Normally, you will see the last post function in the list firing **Generic Event**.

4. Hover your mouse over the post function and click on the edit icon (it looks like a pencil).

5. Select the new `Issue Approved` event and click on **Update**, as shown in the following screenshot. This will make the transition fire our event instead of the default **Generic Event**:

Update parameters of the Fire Event Function for this transition.

Update parameters of the Fire Event Function for this transition.

Event: | Issue Approved |

The event to fire.

Update   Cancel

Let's see how the steps work.

How it works...

Jira's email templates use the Apache Velocity (http://velocity.apache.org) template language to display dynamic data. Each template is a mix of static text (with or without HTML markups) and some Velocity code. If you do not need to have dynamic contents, then you can only have static text in your templates.

In our previous examples, every time you see the dollar sign ($), such as in the phrase $issue.key, it is a piece of Velocity code. The $ sign is an instruction to get a variable from the Velocity context, and the variable name is the word that comes directly after the $ sign so, in this case, it is issue. The period character (.) is an instruction to get the specified value from the variable. So, $issue.key can be read as *get the value of key from the variable issue*, or in other words, *get me the issue's key*.

Jira exposes a number of variables in its Velocity context for email templates; you can find the full list at https://confluence.atlassian.com/display/JIRA041/Velocity+Context+for+Email+Templates.

So, if we take a look at our templates, for the subject template, the ($issue.key) $issue.summary Velocity code will be turned into something like IT-10 Request for Jira administrator access, where IT-10 replaces $issue.key and Request for Jira administrator access replaces $issue.summary.

You can also have conditional logic in your Velocity templates. In our example, we have an if/else condition. We check to see if there is a comment accompanying the approve transition, and if there is, we will display the comment. If there is no comment, then we simply display **No Comment** in italic font.

The following screenshot shows a sample email generated from the custom template that we have created, displayed in Gmail:

Now, onto the custom **Issue Approved** event. Unlike system events, custom events can only be fired from workflow transitions (or custom script code), so we have to update our workflows. Every workflow transition fires an event, and by default, the **Generic Event** is fired. This means that most workflow transitions will have the same notification recipient using the email template.

By configuring the workflow to fire our own custom event, we have finer control over who receives notifications and which templates to use.

Disabling outgoing notifications

This recipe shows you how to completely prevent Jira from sending out emails. You may need to do this if you are performing testing, performing data migration, or cloning a new development instance, and do not want to flood users with hundreds of test notifications.

How to do it...

Go through the following steps to disable outgoing notifications in Jira:

1. Navigate to **Administration** > **System** > **Outgoing Mail**.
2. Click on the **Disable Outgoing Mail** button.

Once you have disabled outgoing mail, Jira will no longer send out notifications. If you want to re-enable outgoing mail, simply click on the **Enable Outgoing Mail** button, and Jira will start sending out emails again.

Creating mail handlers to process incoming emails

Jira is not only able to send emails to users, but also to poll and process emails. It can also create issues or add comments to existing issues. When set up correctly, this can be a powerful way to let your users interact with Jira.

In this recipe, we will set up Jira to poll incoming emails so that it can create new issues and add comments to the existing issues. This is useful in a help-desk scenario where customers can write an email to the support email address of the company and let Jira automatically create issues from them.

Getting ready

Since Jira will be polling email from an inbox, you need to have its connection details, including the following:

- The protocol it supports (for example, **POP** or **IMAP**)
- Authentication details

How to do it...

The first step to configure Jira for processing incoming email is to set up the inboxes that Jira will use to poll the email from:

1. Navigate to **Administration** > **System** > **Incoming Mail**.
2. Click on the **Add POP / IMAP mail server** button.
3. Enter a name for the new mail server. We will be using this when adding the mail handler later.

4. Provide the credentials and click on the **Test Connection** button to make sure that Jira is able to connect to the mail server. If the test is successful, click on the **Add** button. After we have set up the mail inbox, we can set up what are known as mail handlers in Jira to poll and process email. In this recipe, we will use the most common handler to create and/or comment on issues from email contents.

5. Click on the **Add incoming mail handler** button.

6. Enter a name for the mail handler.

7. Select the mail server you just added from the **Server** drop-down list.

You can use the **Local Files** option to test your configuration. This allows you to place a test email on the filesystem so that you do not have to send test emails all the time.

8. Set the **Delay** timer in minutes for how often the handler should poll for new emails. Generally, you should not set the time too short: 5 minutes is usually a good delay.

9. Select the `Create a new issue or add a comment to an existing issue` handler.

10. Click on the **Next** button to configure the mail handler, as shown in the following screenshot:

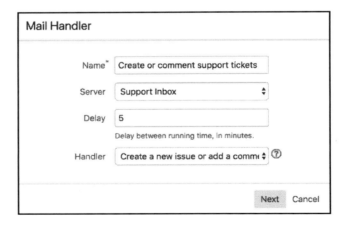

11. Enter the mail handler configuration details. The most important configurations are as follows:
    - **Project**: You can only select one project. All emails from the inbox will go into the selected project.
    - **Issue Type**: This is the issue type from which new issues will be created.
    - **Create Users**: Check this if you want to automatically create a new account based on the email addresses. Note that this will count toward your license seat.
    - **Default Reporter**: If you do not want to create new accounts, you can select an existing user who will be the reporter for all new issues created from emails.

12. Click on the **Add** button to create the mail handler.

The following table explains the various parameters that you need to set:

Parameter	Description
Project	This is where the project's new issues will be created. Note that this is only used for creating new issues. While adding comments, this is ignored, as comments will be added to the issue key specified in the subject.
Issue Type	This is the issue type for all newly created issues.
Strip Quotes	If this option is checked, the text wrapped in quotes will not be used as an issue description or comment.
Catch Email Address	An email with the specified address will be processed if this option is selected.
Bulk	This option dictates how to process autogenerated emails, such as an email from Jira. This is to prevent the creation of a loop where Jira sends email to the same inbox that it is polling the email from.
Forward Email	This option sets an address to which Jira can forward all the emails that it cannot process.
Create Users	This option creates a new user if the sender's email address cannot be found.
Default Reporter	This option sets the user who will be used as the reporter if the sender's email address cannot be found.
Notify Users	Uncheck this option if you do not want Jira to send an account-related email.
CC Assignee	Check this option if you want the first user in the CC list to be the issue's assignee if a matching account can be found.
CC Watchers	Check this option if you want to add the CC list as watchers to the issue if matching accounts can be found.

The following screenshot shows these parameters:

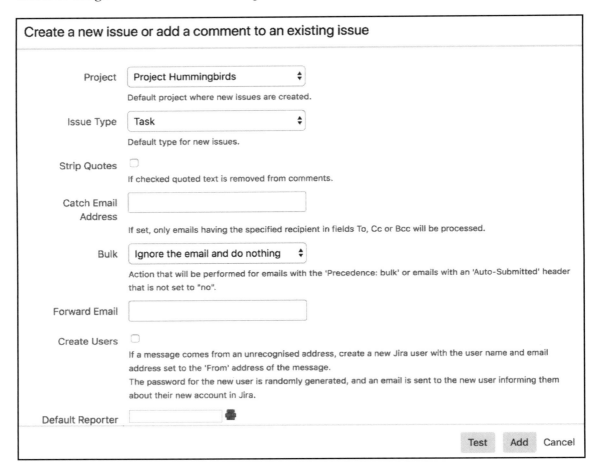

It's time to see the working information.

How it works...

Mail handlers periodically poll for new emails from the selected incoming mail server and process them based on the handler used. The **Create a new issue or add a comment to an existing issue** handlers will create a new issue in Jira, where the email subject becomes the issue summary and the email body becomes the issue description. If the email subject contains an issue key to an existing issue, the email body will be added as a comment to the issue.

- **Add a comment from the non-quoted email body**: This adds the email body that is not quoted with the > or | symbols as a comment to an existing issue.

- **Add a comment with the entire email body**: This adds the entire email body as a comment to an existing issue.

- **Create a new issue from each email message**: This always creates a new issue from an email.

- **Add a comment before a specified marker or a separator in the email body**: This adds the email body *before* a marker line is specified as a regular expression. Contents *after* the marker will be ignored. This is useful when you do not want to include old contents from a forwarded email. Depending on the email client being used, you will need to use regular expressions (regex) to work out the text to be excluded. For most cases, the following regex will work:

  ```
  /From: *|____.*|On .*wrote:|----Orig.*|On
  .*(JIRA).*/
  ```

Using email to update Jira issues

Jira's out-of-the-box mail handlers mostly focus on creating new issues from emails or adding comments to existing issues, based on certain matching criteria. In this recipe, we will look at how to update an existing issue via email.

Getting ready

For this recipe, we need to have the **Enterprise Mail Handler for Jira (JEMH)** app installed. You can download the app from `https://marketplace.atlassian.com/plugins/com.javahollic.jira.jemh-ui`.

How to do it...

Once you have the app installed, the first step is to create a profile. You can think of a profile as a configuration scheme in Jira, such as a workflow scheme. The profile contains all aspects of the configuration settings that are needed for processing incoming emails. To create a new profile, go through the following steps:

1. Navigate to **Administration** > **Manage apps** > **Configure JEMH**.
2. Select the **Profiles** option from the left-hand navigation panel.
3. Click the **Create Profile** button.
4. Enter a name for the profile, select DEVELOPMENT in the **Readiness** field, and click **Create Profile:**

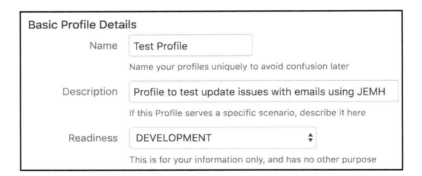

With the profile created, we now need to configure it so that the JEMH app will know how to process incoming emails. The first step is to create an incoming mail handler by going through the following steps:

1. Navigate to **Administration** > **System** > **Incoming Mail**.
2. Click on the **Add incoming mail handler** button.
3. Enter a name for the new mail handler.
4. Select the **Enterprise Mail Handler (JEMH) for Jira** as the **Handler** option and click **Next**.

5. Select the JEMH profile we have just created and click **Submit**:

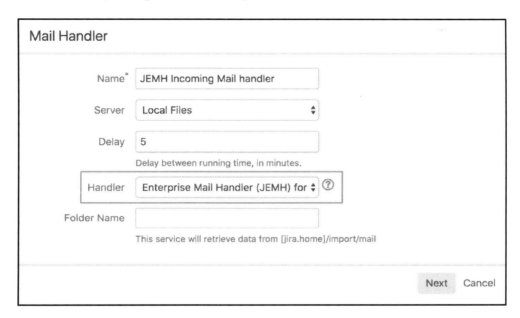

So now that we have an incoming mail handler that is associated with our JEMH profile, the next step is to configure it to process our email content:

1. Click on the **Configure** link for our JEMH profile.
2. Select the **Field Processors** option.
3. Enable the **Colon Suffix (Mailform)** option.
4. Click the **Save** button.

You may choose any format or combination of formats for field processors, and it is usually a good idea to enable multiple processors so that Jira can understand and process more than one. The important point here is that, whichever option you choose, you need to communicate this with your end users so they will understand how to craft their emails so that they can be successfully processed by Jira.

Look at the following screenshot:

Field Processors

Field Processors analyse email content and extract text which is then converted to Directives

Processor Name	Description	Enabled
Basic	no-op mail processor, no directives possible	✓
At(@) Prefix	Keys are prefixed with @, eg @key = value	✗
Colon Suffix (Mailform)	Keys are suffixed with :, eg Some Key: value	✓

This is the minimum required configuration to set up an incoming mail handler so that you can update your issues with emails. With all the configurations in place, the easiest way to test things out is to use the test case feature provided by the app, which avoids the need to send a real email around to all interested users. We can set this up by going through the following steps:

1. Select the **Test Cases** option from the left-hand navigation panel.
2. Click on the **Create** button.
3. Replace the **Subject** with the key of an existing issue in the **Content** textbox.
4. Add the following content under the **Content** textbox:

```
summary: This is a new updated summary
description: This issue is updated via an email.
```

5. Click the **Update and run** button.

You should now see the result of running the test case:

Audit Event ID	20	Cc	
Test Case ID	1	Subject	TEST-24
Date processed	Saturday 20th April @ 15:06	Attachments	0
Profile	Test Profile	Message size	56 B
Updated issues	**TEST-24**	Field processor	ColonSuffix (key:value)
Status	SUCCESS	Filter Name	
From	patrick@appfusions.com	Filter Action	
To	project-x@company.com	Mailbox Action	READ Email will be removed/marked as read...

As shown in the previous screenshot, and the issue you have referenced in the test case would have its summary and description values changed to the preceding content.

How it works...

The JEMH profile contains all the configurations needed for the app to process emails. By creating an incoming mail handler and selecting **Enterprise Mail Handler for Jira (JEMH)** as the handler, Jira will be able to pass on the processing to the JEMH app.

The one key configuration in our recipe is the field processors. The field processor determines how email content should be processed, which directly determines the format for our emails if we want them to be processed correctly. JEMH comes with several processors, and we have chosen to use the **Colon Suffix** processor, which has the format of `key:value`. So in our test-case email, we have the name of the field we want to update as the key and the new value we want to assign to the field as the value—for example, `summary: this is a new summary`.

Setting up a project-specific From email address

By default, all notifications sent from Jira will have the same **From** address, configured as a part of the outgoing mail server; however, it is possible to override this at the project level so that each project can have its own **From** address. This can be very useful if you want to let users reply directly to notifications and have the reply added as a comment.

How to do it...

Go through the following steps to set up a project-specific **From** address:

1. Browse to the project from which you want to set up a specific **From** address.
2. Click on the **Project settings** option.

3. Click on the pencil (edit) icon for the **Email in Notifications** section, as shown in the following screenshot:

4. Enter the email address dedicated to the project.
5. Click on **Update** to apply the changes.

You can revert to the default values by leaving the field blank.

Integrations with Jira

7

Organizations are adopting more and more IT applications, both on-premises and through cloud-based applications, in order to support their various business functions. As today's world is becoming more and more interconnected, these applications need to be similarly interlinked. Business functions often need to work together in order to achieve the desired outcome more efficiently. For this reason, the ability to integrate Jira with other applications has become ever more important.

You can integrate applications with Jira in many ways, both when reaching out to obtain data from other systems and when allowing other systems to access Jira's own data. Jira comes with support to integrate with other Atlassian applications and a number of other popular cloud applications, such as GitHub. Other than the integration supported out of the box, there are also many third-party apps that provide integration with applications and platforms such as Google Drive, Slack, and more. Lastly, there is **webhook**, a relatively new approach that allows any other application to register with Jira for callbacks when certain events occur.

In this chapter, we will cover the following recipes:

- Integrating Jira with Confluence
- Integrating Jira with other Jira instances
- Integrating Jira with Bamboo for build management
- Integrating Jira with Bitbucket Server
- Integrating Jira with Bitbucket Cloud and GitHub

- Integrating Jira with Slack
- Integrating Jira with Google Drive
- Using Jira webhooks
- Using the Jira REST API

Integrating Jira with Confluence

You will often use Jira to track the progress of your engineering projects, using another application to keep the documentation for these projects. In this recipe, we will look at how to integrate Jira with Confluence, which is another popular application from Atlassian that is commonly used for documentation.

Getting ready

Since we will be using Confluence in this recipe, you will need to have an instance of Confluence running on your system. If you do not have one, you can download a free Confluence trial from `https://www.atlassian.com/software/confluence`.

How to do it...

The first step is to establish the link between Jira and Confluence:

1. Navigate to **Administration** > **Applications** > **Application links** in Jira.
2. Enter your Confluence URL into the **Application** textbox and click the **Create new link** button. Jira should automatically detect the target application as Confluence. If, for some reason, it does not, make sure you select **Confluence** as the **Application** type when prompted, as shown in the following screenshot:

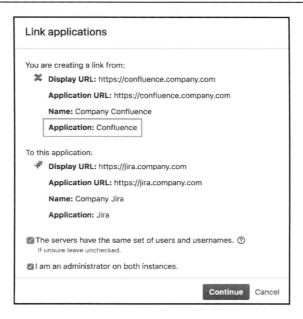

We also need to enable the **Remote access API** (disabled by default) in Confluence:

1. Log in to **Confluence** as a Confluence administrator.
2. Navigate to **Administration** > **Further Configuration**.
3. Click on **Edit**, scroll down, and check the **Remote API (XML-RPC & SOAP)** option.
4. Click on **Save** to apply the change:

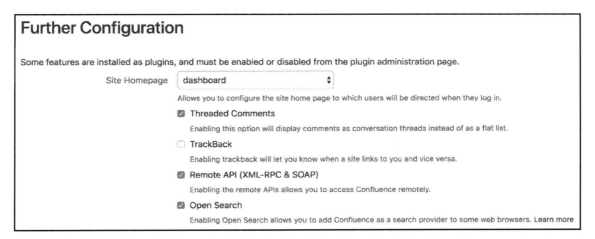

The remote access API is now enabled.

How it works...

Once we have linked Jira with Confluence, there will be a new option called **Confluence Page**, which appears when you select the **Link** option in the **More issue** menu, as shown in the following screenshot:

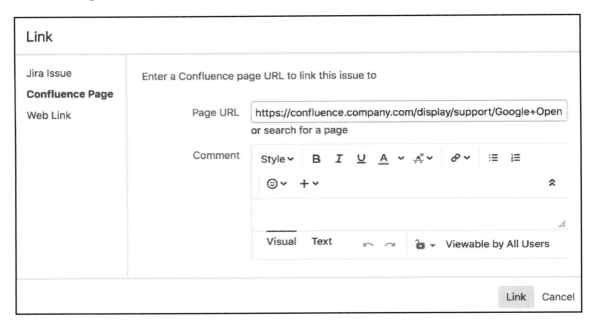

If you know the exact URL of the Confluence page, you can enter it in the **Page URL** field, or click on the **search for a page** link and search for the page you want to link to:

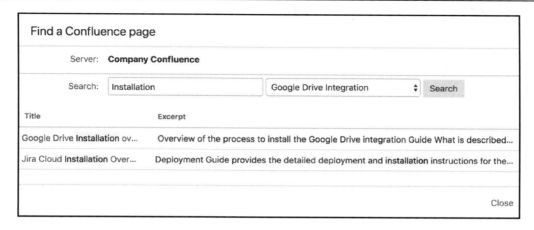

Once you have found the page you want, simply click on it, and then click on the **Link** button. You will see a page similar to the one shown in the following screenshot:

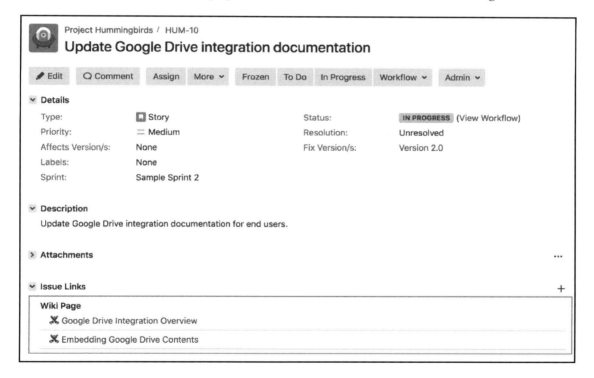

As you can see, the linked pages will be shown under the **Issue Links** section in the **Wiki Page** category.

Integrating Jira with other Jira instances

If you have multiple Jira instances in your organization, it is sometimes useful to integrate them with each other, especially when teams from different projects need to collaborate and work together. In this recipe, we will integrate two Jira instances with each other so that we can link issues across systems.

How to do it...

Go through the following steps to link two Jira instances together:

1. Navigate to **Administration** > **Applications** > **Application links**.
2. Enter the other Jira instance's URL and create the application link. Jira should automatically detect the target application as Jira, as shown in the following screenshot:

If, for some reason, Jira does not detect this, make sure you select **Jira** as the **Application** type when prompted

How it works...

Once you have integrated two Jira instances with each other using an application link, you will be able to search for and link issues from the remote Jira instance to issues in the local Jira instance. Look at the following screenshot:

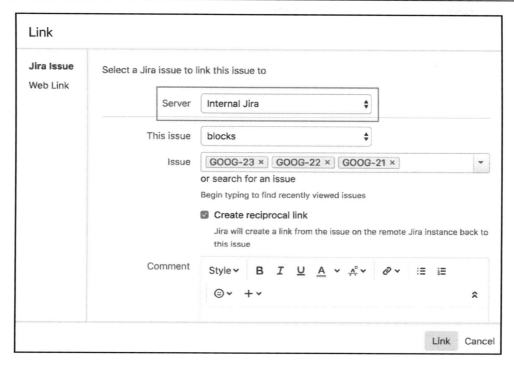

As you can see, when you use the link feature, Jira will prompt you to select the Jira instance that you want to search for issues to link with.

Integrating Jira with Bamboo for build management

Bamboo is the continuous integration and build server from Atlassian. If your development team is using Jira, then it makes perfect sense to also use Bamboo and integrate the two together.

Getting ready

Since we will be using Bamboo in this recipe, you will need to have a Bamboo instance running. If you do not have one, you can download a free Bamboo trial from `https://www.atlassian.com/software/bamboo`.

How to do it...

Since we are connecting to another Atlassian application here, we should take advantage of the application links:

1. Navigate to **Administration** > **Applications** > **Application links**.
2. Enter your Bamboo URL and create the application link. Jira should automatically detect the target application as Bamboo, as shown in the following screenshot:

If, for some reason, Jira does not detect this, make sure you select Bamboo as the Application type when prompted.

How it works...

Once you have integrated Jira and Bamboo, you will be able to run and release build plans directly from Jira. All you have to do is select the version to release and select the new **Build and Release** option, as shown in the following screenshot:

From the release dialog shown in the following screenshot, you can select which build plan to use and run the build by clicking on the **Release** button. If the build is successful, Jira will automatically mark the version as released once the build is completed:

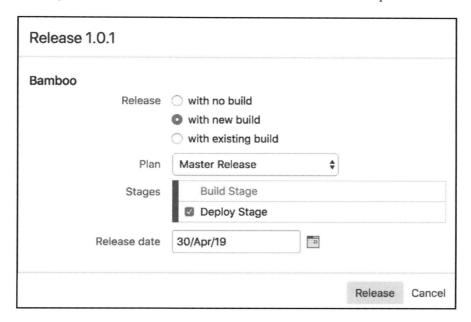

Another feature that you get from integration is that you will be able to see a list of builds that are related to a given Jira issue from the **Development** issue panel:

As you can see, all the build are now listed.

There's more...

Apart from Bamboo, Jira also supports other build server systems, such as Jenkins and Hudson, via third-party apps. You can get the app for Jenkins and Hudson from `https://` `marketplace.atlassian.com/plugins/com.marvelution.jira.plugins.jenkins`.

After you have installed the app, there will be two new application types to choose from while creating new application links—namely, Jenkins and Hudson.

Integrating Jira with Bitbucket Server

Bitbucket is the on-premises enterprise Git source code management tool. It is another application from Atlassian that provides you with all the great **distributed version control system** (**DVCS**) features and benefits. If you are using Jira for software development projects, then you should consider Bitbucket for your version control needs.

In this recipe, we will integrate Jira with Bitbucket Server so that developers can see what changes are made to a given issue.

Getting ready

Since we will be using Bitbucket Server in this recipe, you need to have a Bitbucket Server instance running on your system. If you do not have one, you can download a free Bitbucket Server trial from `https://www.atlassian.com/software/bitbucket`.

How to do it...

Go through the following steps to integrate Jira with Bitbucket Server:

1. Navigate to **Administration** > **Applications** > **Application links**.
2. Enter your Bitbucket Server URL and create the application link. Jira should automatically detect the target application as Bitbucket, as shown in the following screenshot:

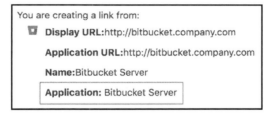

If, for some reason, Jira does not detect it, make sure you select Bitbucket Server as the Application type when prompted

How it works...

Jira and Bitbucket Server integration work by looking through your *commit logs* for comments that start with or contain any issue keys. See the following screenshot:

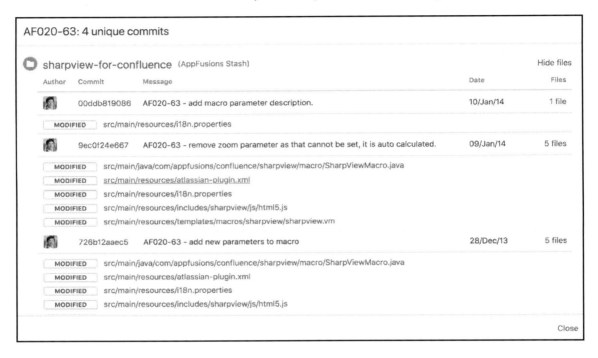

If the commit comment contains an issue key, the commits will be displayed in the **Development** issue panel of the issue.

There is more...

If you are using Bitbucket Cloud instead of running it on-premises, refer to the next recipe for information on how to integrate with it.

Integrating Jira with Bitbucket Cloud and GitHub

Bitbucket Cloud is Atlassian's cloud-based code repository service. It provides public and private code repositories, with support for both Git and Mercurial. It is a great option for organizations that want to move to DVCS, but do not want to deal with the infrastructure overhead.

In this recipe, we will look at how to integrate our on-premises-hosted Jira with Bitbucket in the cloud.

Getting ready

Since we will be using Bitbucket Cloud in this recipe, you need to have a Bitbucket account (both Git and Mercurial repositories will work). If you do not have one, you can sign up for a free account at `https://bitbucket.org`.

How to do it...

The first step is to create a new consumer in Bitbucket Cloud for Jira, which will generate the consumer key and secret:

1. Log in to your Bitbucket account.
2. Navigate to **Bitbucket settings** > **OAuth**.
3. Click on the **Add consumer** button under **OAuth consumers**.
4. Enter a name for the new OAuth consumer. The name you enter here will be displayed when Jira requests access authorization, so you should use a name that is easily understandable, such as `Atlassian Jira`.

5. Click on **Save**. This will generate the consumer details we need for the next step:

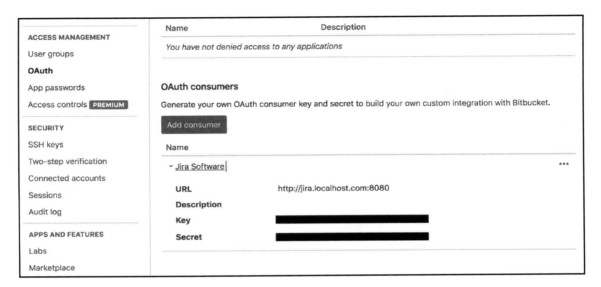

Once we have created the new consumer, the next step is to enter the consumer key and secret details into Jira, as follows:

1. Navigate to **Administration > Applications > DVCS Accounts**.
2. Click on the **Link Bitbucket Cloud or GitHub account** button.
3. Select **Bitbucket Cloud** as the **Host** option.
4. Enter the Bitbucket account name, the **OAuth Key**, and the **OAuth Secret** details that are generated from the consumer we just created:

5. Click on **Add** to link Jira to Bitbucket Cloud.

Once Jira has established a connection to Bitbucket Cloud, you will be prompted to grant Jira access to your Bitbucket Cloud account. Make sure the consumer name (in bold) is the same as the consumer we created, and then click on **Grant access**:

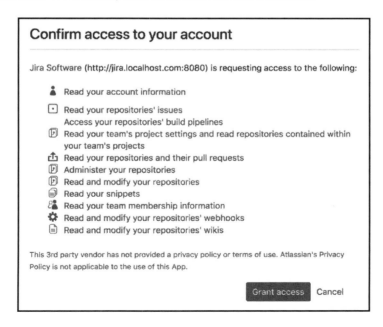

Let's understand how these steps work.

How it works...

Jira uses OAuth as the authorization mechanism to retrieve data from Bitbucket. With OAuth, the application that retrieves data is called the **consumer**, and the application that provides data is called the **provider**.

Each consumer needs to be registered with the provider, that generates a key or secret pair. We performed the registration in our first step by adding a new consumer in Bitbucket:

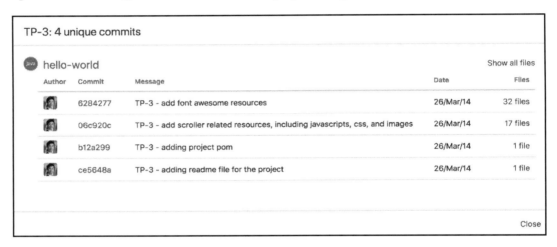

If you do not see the **Development** issue panel, make sure you have the **View Development Tools** project permission.

 By default, members of the **Developers** project role have the **View Development Tools** permission.

There's more...

As you might have already seen during the setup process, Jira also supports GitHub, both the standard cloud version and the enterprise on-premises version. To integrate with GitHub, you follow the same steps; however, while setting up DVCS accounts, you need to select GitHub instead of Bitbucket.

With GitHub, you will also need the consumer key and secret that is generated when you register a new application in GitHub. You can register the application as follows:

1. Log in to your GitHub account.
2. Navigate to **Account settings** > **Developer settings**.
3. Select the **OAuth Apps** tab:

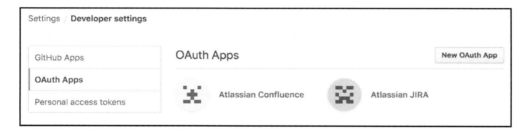

4. Click on **New OAuth App** and enter a name.
5. Enter Jira's URL for both the **Homepage URL** and **Authorization callback URL**.
6. Click on **Register application**.

After you have registered the application, a new client key and secret pair will be generated for Jira to use. You then just need to go to Jira's DVCS account section and select **GitHub** as the host when linking a new DVCS account to Jira.

Integrating Jira with Slack

Slack is the world's most popular cloud-based collaboration tool. It provides features such as persistent chat rooms, file sharing, direct messaging, and much more, with support for web, desktop, and mobile. Atlassian has formed a strategic partnership with Slack, committing to better integration between the two companies' products and services.

In this recipe, we will integrate Jira with Slack so that every time an issue is created or updated in Jira, a notification will be sent to the corresponding Slack channel.

Getting ready

Since we will be using Slack in this recipe, you will need to have a Slack account. If you do not have one, you can sign up for a free account at `https://slack.com`.

The integration requires the **Jira Server for Slack (Official)** app, which is the official app from Atlassian. You can get the app from `https://marketplace.atlassian.com/apps/1220099/jira-server-for-slack-official`.

How to do it...

Go through the following steps to integrate Jira with Slack:

1. Navigate to **Administration** > **Applications** > **Slack**.
2. Click on the **Connect Slack team** button.
3. Choose the recommended **Basic** option and click on the **Go to Slack** button, which will take you to Slack:

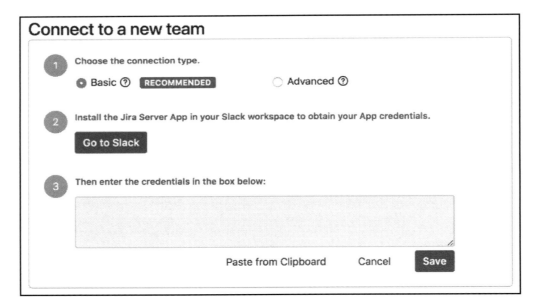

4. Log in to Slack (if you are not logged in already) and install the Jira Server Slack app.
5. Authorize access when prompted:

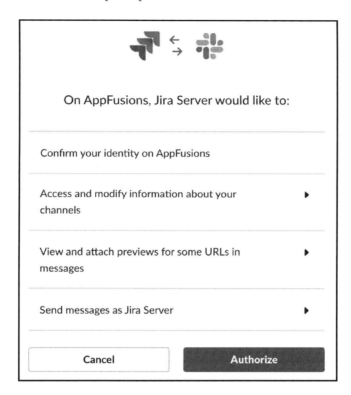

On AppFusions, Jira Server would like to:

Confirm your identity on AppFusions

Access and modify information about your channels ▶

View and attach previews for some URLs in messages ▶

Send messages as Jira Server ▶

Cancel   Authorize

6. Go back to Jira and check that the credentials textbox is automatically filled in with your Slack's details.
7. Click on the **Save** button and the integration will be established between Jira and Slack.

Once you have completed the integration setup, you can connect your Jira projects with Slack channels, as shown in the following screenshot, where we have enabled notifications to be sent to the #hummingbird channel regarding all activities on issues in the Project Hummingbirds project:

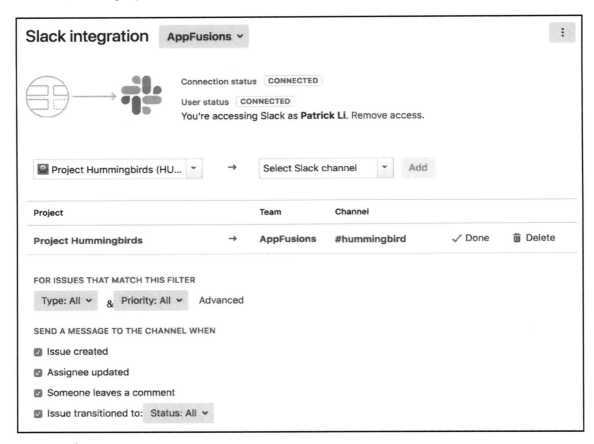

After you have linked your Jira project to a Slack channel, changes to issues will appear in Slack. The integration also includes a number of commands you can run in Slack; simply type in /jira and Slack will prompt you with a list of options:

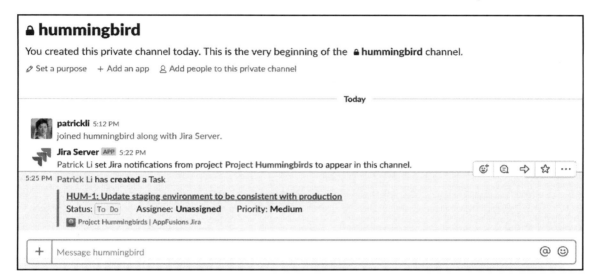

Other than the official Slack integration app from Atlassian, there are also other third-party apps on the Atlassian Marketplace with different features you can try. This is one of the strengths of Jira: there are always other options if the default does not fit your needs, and if all else fails, you also have the option to create your own.

Integrating Jira with Google Drive

It is common for organizations today to use some kind of document-management system—either on-premises or in the cloud—such as Google Drive, Box, and Dropbox.

In this recipe, we will integrate Jira with Google Drive so that users will be able to search, link, preview, and download files stored in Google Drive from Jira.

Getting ready

For this recipe, we need to have Google Drive installed in the Atlassian Jira app. You can download it from `http://www.appfusions.com/display/GDOCSJ/Home` and install it with the UPM.

How to do it...

Go through the following steps to set up an integration between Jira and Google Drive:

1. Go to `https://console.developers.google.com/project` and follow the instructions from `https://developers.google.com/identity/protocols/OAuth2` to create a new OAuth client.
2. Copy the Google OAuth client ID and secret from the generated OAuth client.
3. Navigate to **Administration** > **Manage apps** > **Google Configuration**.
4. Enter the Google OAuth client ID and secret into the **Client ID** and **Client Secret** fields, respectively.
5. Click the **Save** button to complete the set up.

The following table shows the fields on the **Google Configuration** page:

Field	Description
Client ID	The Google OAuth2 client ID
Client secret	The Google OAuth2 client secret

The **Google Configuration** page is displayed in the following screenshot:

Let's see how these steps work.

How it works...

The integration of Google Drive with Jira uses OAuth, where each user needs to first authorize Jira to access Google Drive on their behalf. This process is called the **OAuth dance**.

Once the app is installed and configured, there will be a new **Link Google Document** field under the **More** menu that can be seen while viewing issues. Clicking on that option will present you with a dialog to either browse or search for files stored in Google Drive. You can then select the files you want to link with by checking the appropriate checkboxes:

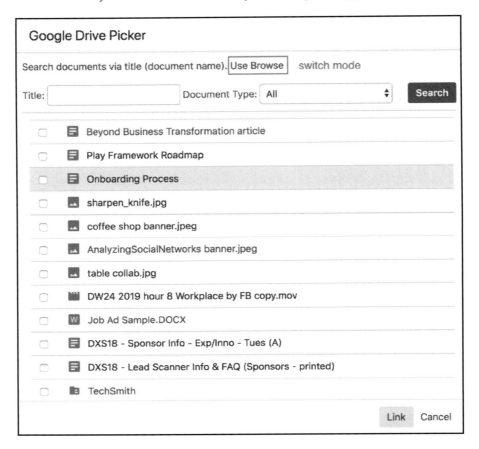

After you have selected and linked the files you want, the selected files will be listed under the **Issue Links** section:

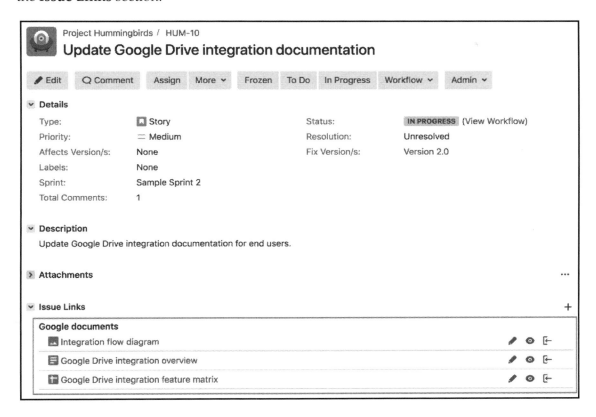

Depending on the file type, you will be able to view, edit, and download the native Google Drive files if you have the required permissions from Google Drive.

There's more...

There are many other third-party integration apps available that support popular cloud vendors, including the following:

- **Salesforce**: The URL is as follows: `https://marketplace.atlassian.com/plugins/com.atlassian.jira.plugin.customfield.crm`.
- **Box**: The URL is as follows: `http://www.appfusions.com/display/BOXJIRA/Home`.

Using Jira webhooks

In previous recipes, we looked at how to integrate Jira with specific applications and platforms. In this recipe, we will look at webhooks, which is a different way of implementing integration with Jira.

How to do it...

Go through the following steps to set up a webhook:

1. Navigate to **Administration** > **System** > **Webhooks**.
2. Click on the **Create a webhook** button.
3. Enter a name for the new webhook. This should clearly explain the purpose of the webhook and/or the target system—for example, `WebHook for Slack #support channel`.
4. Enter the URL of the target system for the webhook to call. The URL should be provided by the target system.
5. Check the **Exclude details** checkbox if adding data to `POST` will cause errors.
6. Enter the **JQL** to define the issues that will trigger the webhook or leave it blank for all issues. It is recommended that you use JQL to restrict the scope.
7. Select the issue events that will trigger the webhook.
8. Click on **Create** to register the webhook:

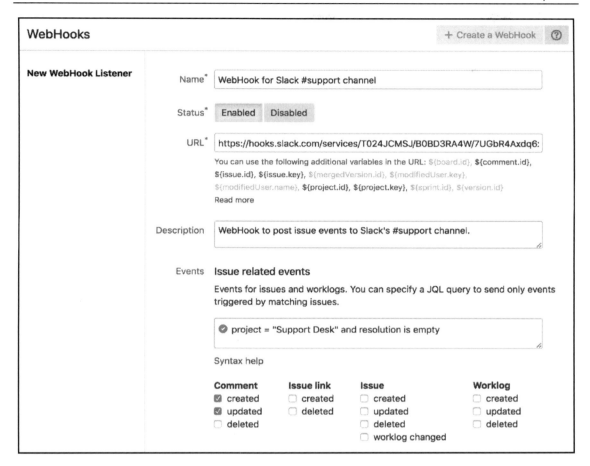

This completes the steps for this recipe.

How it works...

Webhooks use an event-based mechanism, where the source system (in this case, Jira) will make an HTTP `POST` call to all the registered webhooks when a registered event occurs. This is very similar to Jira's internal notification system where emails are sent based on events.

With the event-based approach, instead of requiring the remote application to constantly poll Jira for changes, which is both inefficient and inadequate for situations where changes need to be processed in real time, the remote application can be registered in Jira with a webhook, and Jira will call the application when the event occurs.

There's more...

You can also trigger webhooks from the workflow `POST` function with the `Trigger a Webhook POST` function. All you have to do is select the transition that will be the trigger, add the `POST` function, and select the webhook to be triggered:

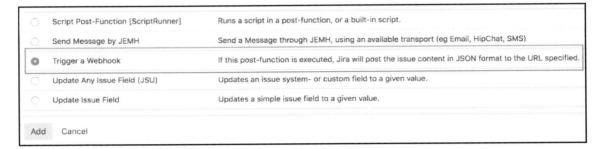

This is particularly useful since the webhook configuration panel only lists some of the basic event types, but not any custom event types that are used in workflows.

Using the Jira REST API

Jira exposes many of its features through a set of REST APIs, allowing other applications to interact with it. With these APIs, you can perform operations such as searching, creating, and deleting issues. In fact, several of the apps used throughout this book make use of these REST APIs to perform their functions.

Being a web-based standard, Jira's REST API allows you to use any technology with it. This means that you can write the code in Java, .NET, JavaScript, or even simple bash scripts.

In this recipe, we will be using the RESTClient Firefox add-on to run a search query against Jira to get a list of issues assigned to the currently logged in user. There are many other tools you can use, such as cURL and Postman for Chrome.

How to do it...

Go through the following steps to run a search query using Jira's REST API:

1. Open up RESTClient in the Firefox browser.
2. Set the **Method** to **GET**.

3. Enter `http://localhost:8080/rest/api/2/search?jql=assignee=curre
ntUser()` into the **URL** textbox. Make sure that you change the URL to your Jira
instance.

4. Select **Basic authentication** and enter your username and password.

5. Click on the **SEND** button.

You should see the result of the API call under the **Response** section. Select the **Preview** tab
to see the result as formatted JSON, as shown in the following screenshot:

The result of the API call is now visible.

How it works...

Jira's REST APIs always follow the URI structure of
`http://host:port/context/rest/api-name/api-version/resource-name`. So, in
our example, we are using version 2 of the search API. The `jql` parameter contains the
actual JQL query we are running. Most APIs will require you to be logged in, so we
configure the settings to use basic authentication as part of our API call.

There's more...

There is an app called **Atlassian REST API Browser (RAB)** that you can install in Jira that allows you to interact with your Jira's REST APIs directly in a browser. You can get this app from `https://marketplace.atlassian.com/plugins/com.atlassian.labs.rest-api-browser/server/overview`.

After you have installed the app, you can open your browser and go to `http://your_jira_instance/plugins/servlet/restbrowser`. You should see an API browser interface similar to the one shown in the following screenshot. On the left-hand side, you will see a full list of the REST APIs that are available in your Jira instance (based on its version):

When you click on any of the APIs, the browser will present you with all the parameters and options available, so you will no longer need to manually find out what they are. This allows you to test and experiment with the APIs quickly, without having to write any code upfront or use any additional tools.

8
Jira Troubleshooting and Administration

In the previous chapters, we looked at Jira's different customization options. As we have seen, Jira can be a complex system, especially as the number of customizations increases. This can be a headache for administrators when users run into problems and require support.

In this chapter, we will how learn to use tools for troubleshooting Jira configuration issues that easily pinpoint the cause of the problem. We will also look at other tools that can help you, as an administrator, to be more efficient at diagnosing and fixing issues, as well as supporting your users.

In this chapter, we will cover the following recipes:

- Troubleshooting notifications
- Troubleshooting permissions
- Troubleshooting field configurations
- Running Jira in safe mode
- Importing data from other issue trackers
- Automating tasks in Jira

- Running scripts in Jira
- Switching user sessions in Jira
- Working with Jira from the command line
- Viewing Jira logs online
- Managing shared filters and dashboards

Troubleshooting notifications

In this recipe, we will look at how to troubleshoot problems related to notifications, such as determining whether a user is receiving notifications for an issue and determining the reason why a user might not be receiving notifications.

How to do it...

Go through the following steps to troubleshoot notification problems in Jira:

1. Navigate to **Administration** > **System** > **Notification Helper**.
2. Select the user that is not receiving the notifications as expected.
3. Select the issue for which the user is expected to receive notifications.
4. Select the notification event that should trigger the notification.
5. Click on **Submit** to start troubleshooting.

You can also run the **Notification Helper** tool from the **Admin** menu while viewing an issue.

How it works...

The **Notification Helper** tool works by looking at the notification scheme settings that are used by the project of the selected issue, and it verifies whether the selected user matches one of the notifications.

Let's take a look at the following screenshot:

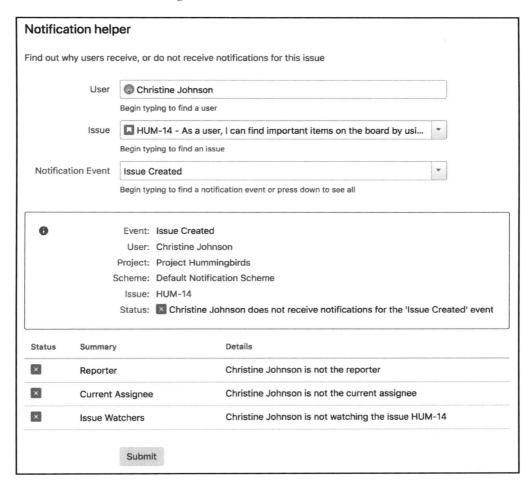

The user, **Christine Johnson**, should not receive notifications about the **HUM-14** issue, because she is not the reporter, assignee, or a watcher of the issue.

There's more...

Of course, other than your notification scheme settings, you will also want to check that your Jira is able to send outgoing emails successfully (refer to the *Setting up an outgoing mail server* recipe in `Chapter 6`, *Emails and Notifications*), and also that the notification emails are not being filtered out to the user's spam folder.

Troubleshooting permissions

In this recipe, we will look at how to troubleshoot problems caused by permission settings, such as a user being unable to view an issue.

How to do it...

Go through the following steps to troubleshoot permission problems in Jira:

1. Navigate to **Administration** > **System** > **Permission Helper**.
2. Select the affected user.
3. Select the issue for which the user is expected to have permissions.
4. Select the permission type that the user should have access to.
5. Click on **Submit** to start troubleshooting.

You can also run the **Permission Helper** tool from the **Admin** menu while viewing an issue.

How it works...

The **Permission Helper** tool works by looking at both the permission scheme and the security scheme settings that are used by the selected issue. It verifies whether the selected user has the required permissions for the necessary action.

As shown in the following screenshot, the user **Eric Lin** does not have the ability to delete the **HUM-10** issue because he does not have the **Administrators project role** for the project:

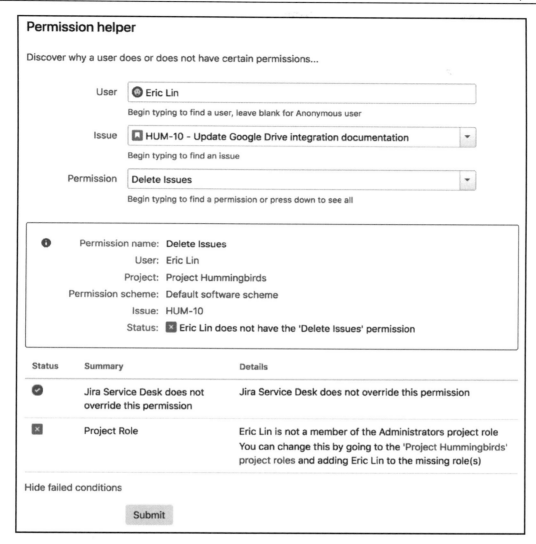

This completes our recipe.

Troubleshooting field configurations

In this recipe, we will determine why a given field is not displayed while viewing an issue and look at how to troubleshoot it.

How to do it...

Go through the following steps to troubleshoot why a field is not being displayed:

1. Navigate to the issue that has missing fields.
2. Select the **Where is my field?** option from the **Admin** menu:

3. Select the field that is missing to start troubleshooting.

How it works...

The **Field Helper** tool examines field-related configurations, including the following:

- **Field context**: This checks whether the field is a custom field. The tool will then check whether the field has a context that matches the current project and issue type combinations.
- **Field configuration**: This verifies that the field is set to **Hidden**.
- **Screens**: This verifies whether the field is placed on the current screen based on the screen scheme and issue type screen scheme.
- **Field data**: This verifies whether the current issue has a value for the field, as custom fields without a value will often not be displayed.

Let's look at the following screenshot:

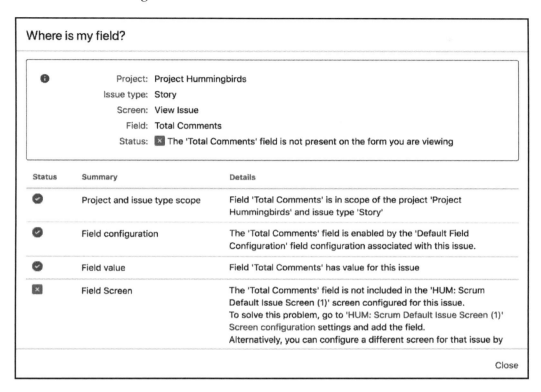

Total Comments is a custom field, and the reason it isn't displayed is that it has not been added to the screen.

Running Jira in safe mode

When you have different people installing apps in Jira, you can, at times, run into problems, but you might be unsure as to which app has caused a certain problem. In these cases, you can use the process of elimination by first disabling all the apps and re-enabling them one at a time.

Getting ready

Enabling safe mode will impact on your users, so make sure you plan accordingly before doing so.

How to do it...

Go through the following steps to enable safe mode:

1. Navigate to **Administration** > **System** > **Manage apps**.
2. Click on the **Enter safe mode** link at the bottom of the page.
3. Click on **Enter safe mode** when you are prompted to confirm the operation.

The window looks like the following screenshot:

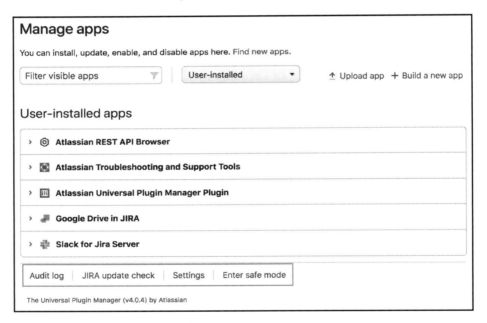

This completes the steps for our recipe.

How it works...

The **Universal Plugin Manager** (**UPM**) is what Jira uses to manage all its apps. Other than being the interface that allows you to upload and install third-party apps (unless instructed otherwise), it also provides a number of other useful administrative features.

When you enable safe mode, the UPM will disable all user-installed apps, which returns Jira to a vanilla state. You can then individually enable each app, thereby finding the problematic app via the process of elimination.

There's more...

The UPM also provides an audit feature, which keeps track of all the changes related to the apps. You can simply click on the **Audit log** link at the bottom of the page and the UPM will display a list of changes made in the last 90 days.

Importing data from other issue trackers

If you have another issue tracker and are thinking about switching to Jira, you can often easily migrate your existing data into Jira with its built-in import tool.

In this recipe, we will look at how to import data from Bitbucket's issue tracker. Jira supports the importing of data from other issue trackers, such as **Bugzilla** and **GitHub**, and as a CSV file. As we will see, the process is almost identical, so this recipe can be applied to these other systems too.

How to do it...

Go through the following steps to import data from other issue trackers, such as Bitbucket, into Jira:

1. Navigate to **Administration** > **System** > **External System Import**.
2. Select the source's issue tracker system. We will select **Bitbucket** for this recipe.

3. Click on the **Next** button to authorize the Jira importer to access data from Bitbucket, and when prompted, click on **Authorize**:

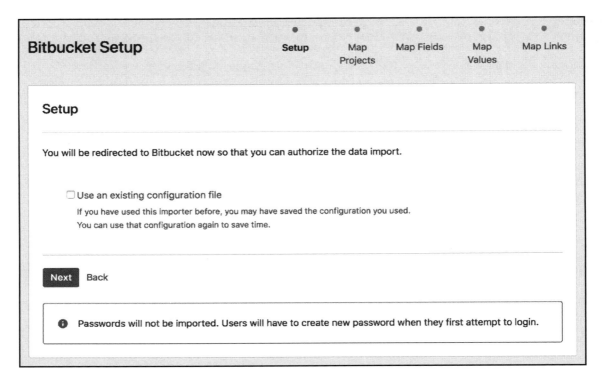

4. Map projects from Bitbucket to Jira projects. Check the **Don't import this project** option for those projects that you do not want to import to Jira. Click on **Next** to continue, as shown in the following screenshot.

5. After you have clicked on **Next**, Jira will query Bitbucket to get an export of settings, such as fields and values, so that they can be used to map the Jira counterparts. This process may take a few minutes, depending on the size of your Bitbucket project:

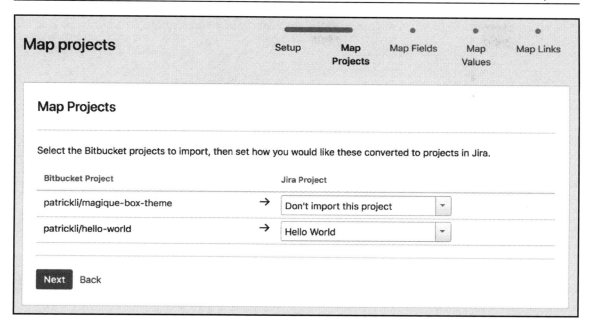

6. Select the fields from Bitbucket that you want to manually map to the Jira field values. Click on **Next** to continue:

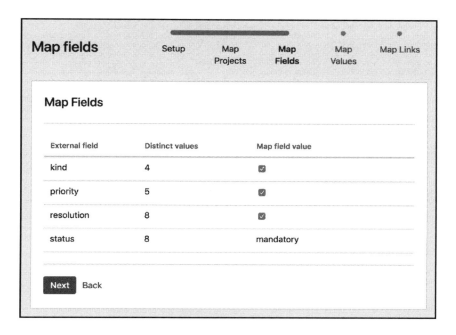

7. Map the field values from Bitbucket to the field values of the Jira fields, as shown in the following screenshot. Click on **Next** to continue:

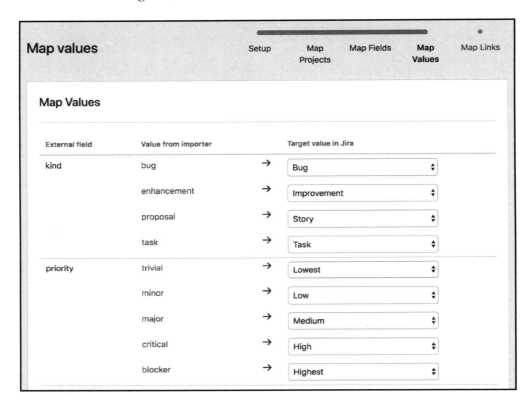

8. Map Bitbucket's link types to the Jira issue link types. Click on **Begin Import** to start importing data into Jira, as seen in the following screenshot:

9. Review the import result. You can click on the **download a detailed log** link to get a full log of the process if the import has failed. You can also click on the **save the configuration** link to get a copy of the mapped files so that you do not have to remap everything from scratch next time:

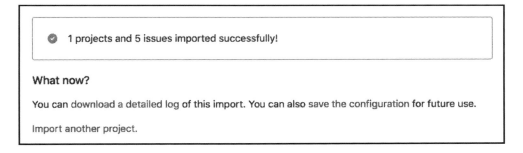

We will now look at how the steps work.

How it works...

Jira has a common wizard interface for all the different issue tracker importers. While each importer is unique in its own way, they all follow the same basic steps, as described in the following list:

- **Configuring the target data source**: This step is where the target issue tracker's data is retrieved. It can be direct database access in the case of Bugzilla or it can be over the internet in the case of Bitbucket.

- **Selecting a project to import to**: This is where we have to choose the issues that are to be imported to either an existing project or a new project.
- **Mapping the target system's fields to Jira fields**: This is where the target issue maps the tracker's fields to the corresponding Jira fields. Custom fields can be automatically created as part of the process.
- **Mapping a target system's field values to Jira field values**: This maps the field data based on the previous field mappings. It is usually required for selecting list-based fields, such as priority, issue status, and custom fields.
- **Mapping the issue link types**: This step is optional depending on whether the target issue tracker supports linking. If it does, those link types will need to be mapped to the Jira issue link types.

Although the Jira importer is able to handle most instances where the data mapping is straightforward, for bigger instances with complex mapping requirements, such as project merging and conditional mapping, it is recommended that you engage an Atlassian Expert (https://www.atlassian.com/resources/experts) to handle the migration rather than relying on the importer alone.

There's more...

If there are no import options available for your issue tracker, you can also try to export your data in CSV format and then use the built-in CSV importer to import the data.

Automating tasks in Jira

As an administrator, being able to automate tasks is often a very important part of your job. You will often need to have some programming skills in order to take advantage of some of the automation facilities provided by Jira out of the box, such as **listeners** and **services**. Luckily, there are now tools that can help you with automation without you needing to know any programming.

In this recipe, we will set up an automated task where Jira will periodically check for issues that have not been updated in 7 days, close them, and add a comment.

Getting ready

For this recipe, we need to have the **Automation for Jira** app installed. You can download it from `https://marketplace.atlassian.com/apps/1215460/automation-for-jira` and install it using the UPM.

How to do it...

Go through the following steps to set up an automated task:

1. Navigate to **Administration** > **System** > **Automation rules**.
2. Click on the **Create rule** button.
3. Select the `Scheduled` trigger for the new automation rule.
4. Enter how often the automation task should run. We want our task to run once every day, so enter `1`.
5. Enter the `project = "Support Desk" and updated <= 7d` JQL query so that the automation task will know which issues it should affect:

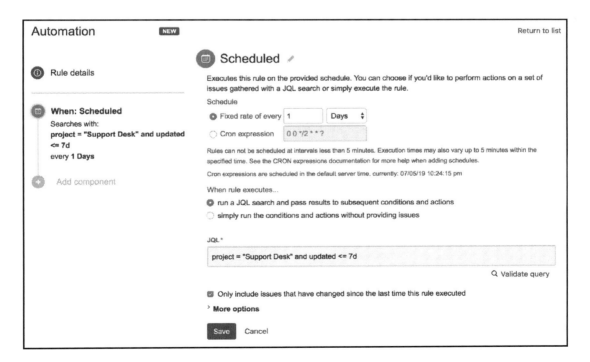

6. Click on the **Save** button to save the trigger configuration.
7. With the trigger configured, we now need to select an action. Since we want to close issues, we will select the **New action** option.
8. Select the **Transition issue** action type.
9. Select the destination status to transition affected issues when the automation task runs. We want to close issues, so select the **Done** status. If your workflow uses a different status, select that instead:

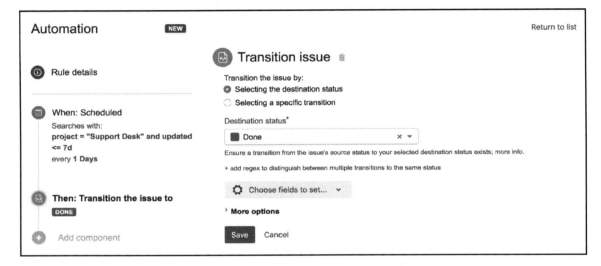

10. If your workflow requires additional fields to be set, you can also set them here by selecting the fields from the **Choose fields to set...** drop-down menu.
11. Click the **Save** button to save our changes.
12. Enter a name for our new automation task, such as **Close old issues**, and click on the **Turn it on** button.

Your completed automation task should look something like the following:

It's time to look at how these steps work.

How it works...

In its most basic form, an automation rule consists of two components: the trigger and the action. The trigger will determine when the automation task will run. There are three built-in trigger types:

- **Issue triggers**: These triggers run when the corresponding issue fires an event, usually when issues are updated in some way, such as during issue updates and workflow transitions.
- **Scheduled**: This trigger type will automatically run on a predetermined time frame. You can use the simple form, as we have in this recipe, to specify the frequency, or you can use a *cron* expression to specify the exact hour, minute, and second.
- **Integrations:** This trigger type creates a webhook URL. When an external system makes an HTTP POST request to the URL, the trigger will run.

The **action** is what will happen when a trigger runs. A trigger can run more than one action. An action can perform operations, including making changes to issue data, sending email notifications, and sending outgoing HTTP POST requests.

You can add more advanced components to your automation rule to have conditional branching and execution. For example, when a trigger is run, you can run one action for issues of type **Bug**, and another action for issues of type **Story**. You can also chain your automation rules so that one rule has a trigger based on a webhook, and you can have another rule with an action that makes an HTTP POST to that webhook URL to trigger it.

With our automation rule, we have set up a trigger to run once every day. We then used a JQL query to select only the issues in the Support Desk project that have not been updated in the last 7 days since the task was run. We then added an action for the trigger to transition all the issues returned from the JQL query to **Done**.

Running scripts in Jira

Jira provides an app framework for people with programming skills to create apps to extend its features or perform tasks that would otherwise be impossible or tedious; however, even with this functionality, it is sometimes overkill to create a full-blown app for what may seem like a simple task. The good news is that there is an option for you to write or program scripts that can take advantage of what the API offers without the burden of full app development.

In this recipe, we will create a Groovy script that will share a number of search filters by adding them as favorites for everyone in Jira—a task that would otherwise take a lot of time if done manually.

Getting ready

For this recipe, we need to have ScriptRunner for the Jira app installed. You can download it from `https://marketplace.atlassian.com/plugins/com.onresolve.jira.groovy.groovyrunner` and install it with the UPM.

How to do it...

Go through the following steps to run a custom Groovy script in Jira (note that you will need to update the filter IDs accordingly):

1. Navigate to **Administration** > **Manage apps** > **Script Console**.
2. Copy the following script into the **Script** text area:

```
import com.atlassian.jira.component.ComponentAccessor
import com.atlassian.jira.favourites.FavouritesManager
import com.atlassian.jira.issue.search.SearchRequest
import com.atlassian.jira.issue.search.SearchRequestManager
import com.atlassian.jira.user.util.UserManager
import com.atlassian.jira.security.groups.GroupManager
import com.atlassian.jira.exception.PermissionException

//Set the filter ID and group to share with here
Long[] searchRequestIds = [10302,10303,10304]
String shareWith = "jira-software-users"
FavouritesManager favouritesManager =
ComponentAccessor.getComponent(FavouritesManager.class)
SearchRequestManager searchRequestManager =
ComponentAccessor.getComponent(SearchRequestManager.class)
UserManager userManager =
ComponentAccessor.getComponent(UserManager.class)
GroupManager groupManager =
ComponentAccessor.getComponent(GroupManager.class)

for(Long searchRequestId in searchRequestIds) {
    SearchRequest searchRequest =
searchRequestManager.getSharedEntity(searchRequestId)
    for (String userName in
groupManager.getUserNamesInGroup(shareWith)) {
        try {
favouritesManager.addFavourite(userManager.getUserByName(userName),
searchRequest)
        } catch (PermissionException e) {
            // the user does not have permission to view this
filter
        }
    }
}
```

3. Switch the filter IDs (searchRequestIds) and group name (shareWith) based on your data. You can get filter IDs by running your filter, and the ID will be in your browser's address bar.

4. Click on **Run** to execute the script.

The **Script Console** window is shown in the following screenshot:

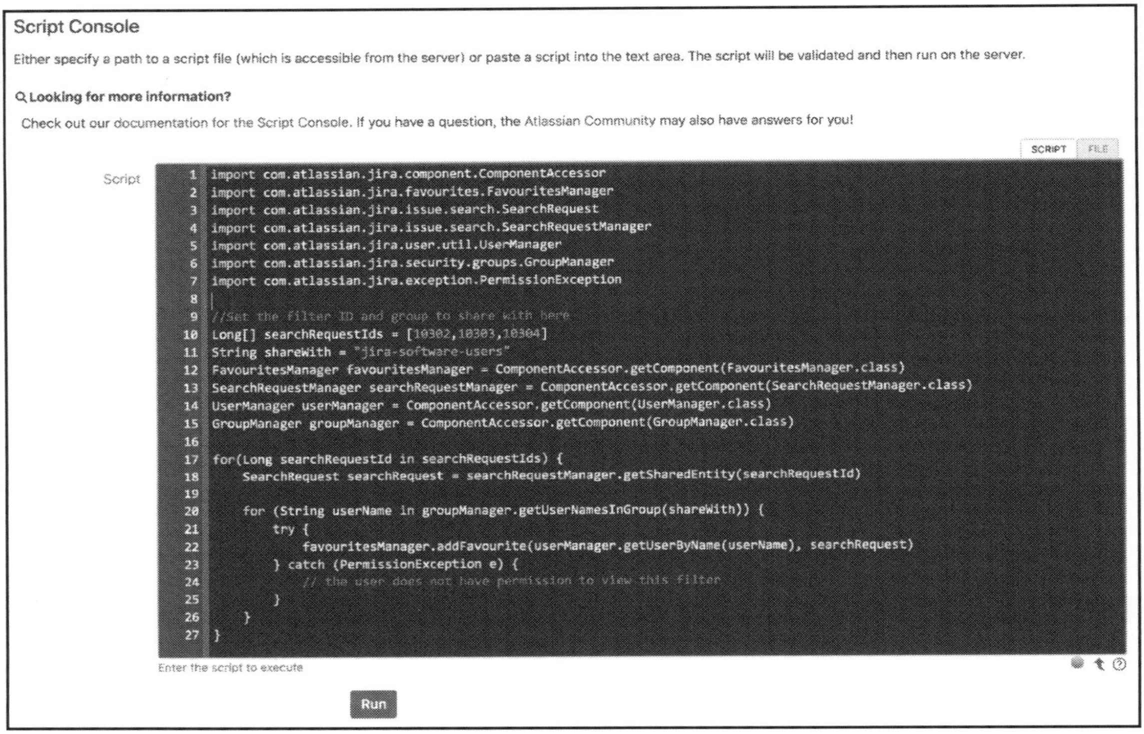

You can see the information being displayed in the console.

How it works...

The ScriptRunner for Jira app allows you to run Groovy scripts inside Jira. Since both Java (what Jira is built with) and Groovy can run on the JVM, you will have access to all the components and APIs that Jira exposes to developers.

In the script, we list a number of search filters by their IDs (these filters need to be shared so that other users can favorite them), loop through them, and add each ID as a favorite to the users in the `jira-software-users` group, all done using Jira's public API.

Switching user sessions in Jira

You will often have problems that only happen to a particular user. In these cases, you will have to either sit next to the user in order to see and understand the problem or reset the user's password and log in as that user.

In this recipe, we will learn how you can switch your current session to any other user's session without having to reset or get hold of the user's password.

Getting ready

For this recipe, we need to have the **SU** (short for **switch user**) for Jira app installed. You can download it from https://marketplace.atlassian.com/plugins/com.dolby. atlassian.jira.jirasu and install it with the UPM.

How to do it...

To switch (**SU**) to a different user, go through the following steps:

1. Navigate to **Administration > User management > Users**
2. Click the **SU** link for the user you want to switch to:

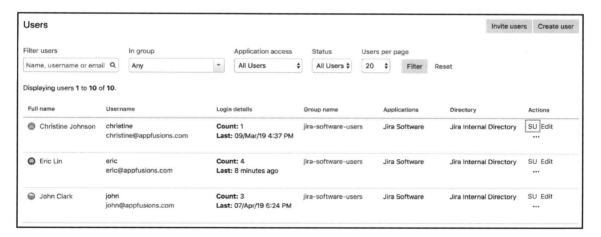

After you have selected the user, your current user session will be switched to that user, with the same configurations and permissions applied. After you are done, you can switch back by selecting the **SU Exit** option from the SU menu item from the top navigation bar.

How it works...

The SU for Jira app works by changing your current user session to the user of your choice, then, from Jira's point of view, you have effectively logged in (without having to supply the user's password) as the selected user.

Now that you understand this, it should be obvious that this technique could be potentially misused in the wrong hands. You can restrict access to the SU functionality by going to the UPM and clicking on the **Configure** button of the SU for Jira app. This will then allow you to restrict access to selected groups.

One useful feature is its audit log. Every time someone uses the SU function, it is logged in the system, so administrators can always go and check if someone has been abusing it. You can access the **SU Audit Log** by navigating to **Administration** > **System** > **SU Audit Log**.

Working with Jira from the command line

We normally interact with Jira via the browser, but sometimes it is useful to be able to use the command line, especially for administrative tasks or writing shell scripts.

In this recipe, we will use the command line to create new users in Jira.

Getting ready

For this recipe, you need to have the **Atlassian Command Line Interface (CLI)** tool available on your workstation. You can download it from `https://marketplace.atlassian.com/plugins/org.swift.atlassian.cli`.

How to do it...

To use the Atlassian CLI tool, we first need to install it by unzipping it to a convenient location on your workstation. Next, update the `jira.sh` (for Unix) or `jira.bat` (for Windows) file to add Jira's details.

For example, as shown in the following command, Jira is running on `http://localhost:8080`, and the administrator credential is `admin_user` with `admin_password` as the password:

```
java -jar 'dirname $0'/lib/jira-cli-3.8.0.jar
-server http://localhost:8080 --user admin_user
--password admin_password "$@"
```

1. So, now that we have everything set up, we can run the following command to create a new user in Jira:

```
./jira.sh --action addUser --userId tester
-userEmail tester@company.com --userFullName
Tester
```

2. You should get the following response:

```
User: tester added with password:
89u66p3mik5q.  Full name is: Tester.  Email is:
tester@company.com.
```

How it works...

The Atlassian CLI tool works by accessing Jira features and functions via its remote SOAP and REST API.

We updated the Jira script file with Jira details, so we don't have to specify them every time; this is useful if we want to use the tool in a script. When we run the Jira script, it will have all the necessary connection information.

The Atlassian CLI comes with a list of command actions, such as the `addUser` action that we used to create users in Jira. You can get a full list of actions from `https://bobswift.atlassian.net/wiki/display/JCLI/Documentation`.

Viewing Jira logs online

Often, when an error occurs, you, as the administrator, will need to examine the Jira log files to pinpoint the exact problem. Normally, in order to get access to the logs, you will need to either SSH into the server or download the file using an FTP client. In a locked-down environment, you will have to request this via your IT team, which could lead to a long turnaround time.

In this recipe, we will look at how you can access and search through your Jira log files, all from the browser.

Getting ready

For this recipe, we need to have the **Last Log for Jira** app installed. You can download it from `https://marketplace.atlassian.com/apps/1211604/last-log-for-jira?hosting=server&tab=overview` and install it with the UPM.

How to do it...

Go through the following steps to access the Jira log files from the browser:

1. Navigate to **Administration** > **Manage apps** > **View log**.
2. Select the log file to view from the **log-file** drop-down.
3. Enter the text string to search the selected log file. If matches are found, they will be highlighted, as shown in the following screenshot:

With this, we have completed the steps for this recipe.

How it works...

Jira writes its logs in the `atlassian-jira.log` file in the `JIRA_HOME/log` directory. Some Jira components, such as Jira Service Desk, and third-party apps write to their own log files. Since the Last Log for Jira app allows you to access all the files inside the `JIRA_HOME/log` directory, you will have access to all the log files.

Managing shared filters and dashboards

Jira allows end users to create their own search filters and dashboards and share them with other users. When the owner of the shared filters and dashboards leaves the organization or goes on leave, others will not be able to make changes to them. In these cases, as the Jira administrator, you can temporarily (or permanently) change the owner of the shared filter and dashboard to a new user.

How to do it...

Go through the following steps to reassign a shared filter or dashboard to another user:

1. Navigate to **Administration** > **System** > **Shared filters** (or dashboards).
2. Search for the shared filter.
3. Select the **Change Owner** option for the filter.
4. Enter a new owner for the filter—for example, yourself—and click on the **Change Owner** button:

This completes the steps for this recipe.

There's more...

Normally, you will only need to change the owner of shared filters or dashboards, as other users use those; however, in rare cases where you need to change the owner of nonshared filters or dashboards, you can first switch the user session to the owner of the filter or dashboard, as outlined in the *Switching user sessions in Jira* recipe, and then change the owner to someone else. Note that this requires the user to be active in Jira, so you might need to first reactivate the account.

Jira Service Desk 9

In previous chapters, we focused on the Jira platform from Atlassian, which is primarily used for issue-tracking purposes. We covered topics such as customizing projects through screens and fields and integrating Jira with other third-party services.

In this chapter, we will look at another closely related Jira product, called Jira Service Desk. This allows you to run a powerful support system, either alongside your engineering projects or independently as an all-purpose support solution. We will look at ways you can customize Jira Service Desk to provide a unique experience for your end users. Since Jira Service Desk is built on top of Jira, its installation procedure is almost identical to that of Jira, and you can refer to the recipes in `Chapter 1`, *Jira Server Administration*, for more details.

In this chapter, we will cover the following recipes:

- Customizing the look and feel of your support portal
- Capturing the right information for service requests from your customers
- Setting up a knowledge base for your customers
- Collaborating with your internal teams on service requests
- Tracking and evaluating performance with a **Service Level Agreement (SLA)**

Customizing the look and feel of your support portal

Jira Service Desk has two main interfaces—one for the customers raising requests and one for the agents providing solutions. In this recipe, we will look at how to customize the service desk portal, which is the frontend user interface used by your customers.

How to do it...

To fully customize your service desk portal, perform the following steps:

1. Log in to **Jira Service Desk** as an administrator.
2. Browse to **Administration** > **Applications** > **Configuration** (under **Jira Service Desk**).
3. Click on the **View and customize** link under **Help Center**.

From here, you can configure a range of customizations for how the service desk portal will look when a customer visits it. You can add a logo, banner, color scheme, and announcement messages. With announcement messages, you can use wiki markup, so you will be able to use styles such as bold and italics and create hyperlinks. For example, the following announcement message uses some of this markup:

```
Welcome to the newly launched Global Support Center!

If you have any issues or questions, please contact us at
help@support.company.com. We are here to help!

_your friendly support team_
```

Your customizations will be reflected as soon as you make the change. Once you are happy with the result, click on the **Save changes** button at the bottom of the screen:

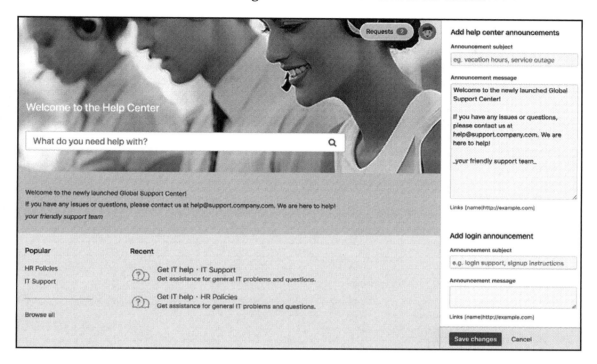

After you have customized the look and feel of your service desk portal, you will need to customize the type of requests that customers can make. By planning out the request types properly, you can help your customers to better understand where to log their requests so that they can be routed to the relevant team members for faster resolution. Request types are managed for each service desk (Jira project):

1. Browse to the service desk that you want to set up request types for.
2. Click on the **Project settings** option in the lower-left corner of the screen.
3. Select the **Request types** option from the panel on the left-hand side panel.
4. Add a new request type by entering the name of the request, its type, and the groups it belongs to. Requests in the same group will be displayed together in the portal. Note that a request can belong to multiple groups.

When selecting and creating groups for your requests, try to name them based on the common theme shared by all the request types that belong to it:

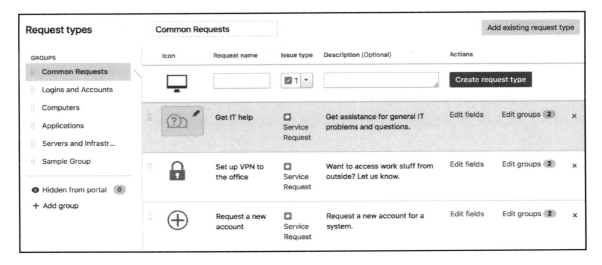

We will now take a look at how this works.

How it works...

Jira Service Desk leverages many of Jira's built-in capabilities, and its request types are built on top of the issue type feature. A request type in a service desk is mapped to an issue type in Jira. The main difference here is that the request type is what the customer sees, so it allows you to give it a more descriptive name to help customers better understand the purpose behind each request type. For example, an issue type called **bug** can have a request type called **report** and an application defect mapped to it. While they will both mean the same thing to a support agent or engineer, the request type will be a lot friendlier in the eyes of a customer.

For this reason, when managing request types, you need to make sure the corresponding issue types exist for the service desk project before you can map to it. You can refer to the *Setting up different issue types for projects* recipe in Chapter 2, *Customizing Jira for Your Projects,* for detailed information:

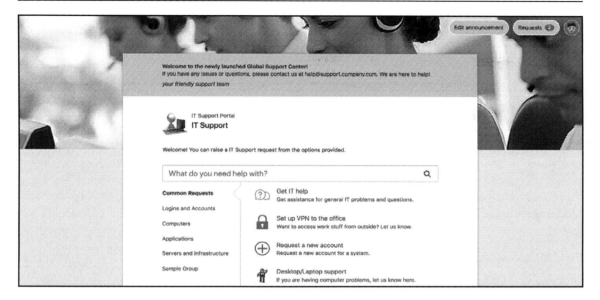

With this, we have completed our recipe.

Capturing the right information for service requests from your customers

In this recipe, we will explore how to customize the screen and field layout for different request types so that you can capture the necessary information from your customers and help your agents to resolve issues quickly. We will also look at setting up different screens and fields for agents so that they can capture additional information independently from the customer's view.

How to do it...

To configure the field layout for the customer portal, perform the following steps:

1. Browse to the service desk to customize the field layout.
2. Click on the **Project settings** option in the lower-left corner.
3. Select the **Request type** option from the panel on the left-hand side.
4. Click on the **Edit fields** link for the request type to configure.

5. Click on the **Add a field** button to add fields to the portal. If you do not see the field you want to add, make sure the field is added to the appropriate screen used by the project:

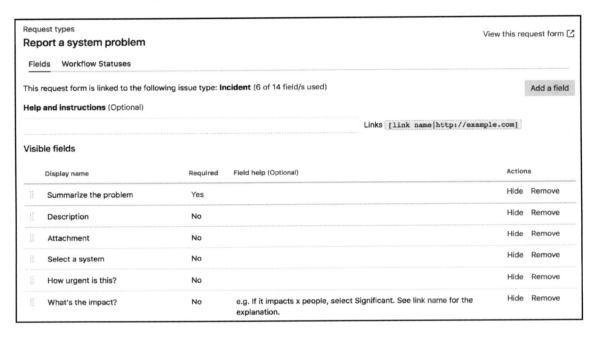

To customize the field layout for agents, you need to configure the screens used for the service desk project. You can refer to the *Setting up customized screens for your projects* recipe in `Chapter 2`, *Customizing Jira for Your Projects,* for detailed information.
The most straightforward method is as follows:

1. Select the **Screens** option from the panel on the left-hand side.
2. Expand the screen scheme for the issue (request) type.
3. Click on the screen for the **View Issue** operation.

4. Search and add the fields that you want to the screen. Fields you add in this way will not be shown to customers unless you specifically add them to the request type, as outlined earlier:

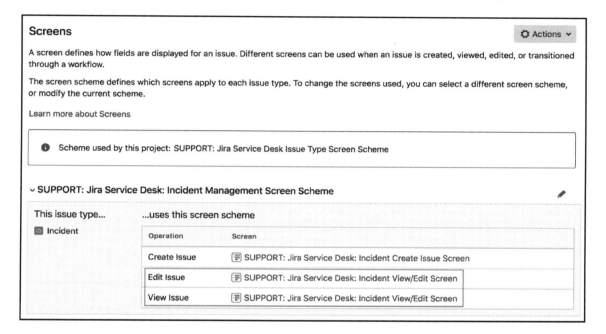

 If your service desk uses different screens for **Edit** and **View**, make sure you make the same changes to the **Edit Issue** screen so that your agents can make changes to those fields.

How it works...

The Jira Service Desk project's field layout is powered by Jira's screen configurations, which include screens, screen schemes, and issue type screen schemes. For the customer portal, Jira Service Desk provides a simplified version of the screen used by the **Create Issue** operation to keep the user experience smooth. This is why, for you to be able to add a field to a request type, the field must first be added to the **Create Issue** operation screen:

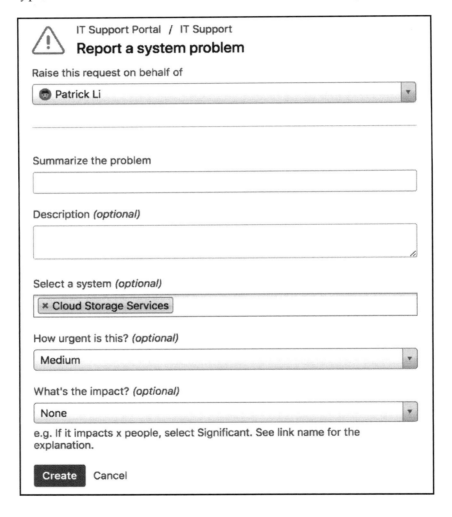

For the agent's view, Jira Service Desk makes full use of Jira's screen and field management features, so you can set up different screens for the **Edit** and **View Issue** operations.

Setting up a knowledge base for your customers

As time progresses, you should start accumulating a wealth of knowledge for common problems faced by customers. It is recommended that you capture this knowledge and make them searchable and indexable through search engines such as Google so that customers can find solutions to these common problems quickly.

In this recipe, we will set up a knowledge base using **Atlassian Confluence** product. By integrating with Confluence, your service desk agents will be able to create articles to capture problem symptoms and solutions based on a set of predefined templates and make them searchable in the service desk.

How to do it...

The first step is to create an application link between Jira and Confluence. You can refer to the *Integrating Jira with Confluence* recipe in `Chapter 7`, *Integrations with Jira*, for detailed information. If you have already integrated Jira and Confluence, you can skip these steps:

1. Browse to the service desk that you want to set up a knowledge base for.
2. Click on the **Project settings** option in the lower-left corner of the screen.
3. Select the **Knowledge base** option from the panel on the left-hand side.

4. Click on the **Set up a link to Confluence** link. If you do not see the following screenshot, then you have already integrated Jira with Confluence, and you can skip this section:

✕ Confluence

Knowledge base

You can link your service desk project to a Confluence knowledge base. Customers can help themselves by searching for knowledge articles from the Customer Portal.

Set up a link to Confluence   Learn more

5. Enter the fully qualified URL for your Confluence instance, and click on the **Create new link** button.
6. Follow the onscreen wizard and complete the setup process.

With the application link in place, we can now go back to the service desk. You should now see the options to link the service desk to a Confluence space.

You may have to refresh your page to see these options after the application link is created.

To set up a Confluence space as a knowledge base for your service desk, perform the following steps:

1. Select the **Link to a Confluence space** option.
2. Select the linked Confluence application from the **Application** drop-down list.
3. Select the space that will become the knowledge base for your service desk. If no space is designated at this point, you can click on the **Create a knowledge base space** link to create a new space on the fly:

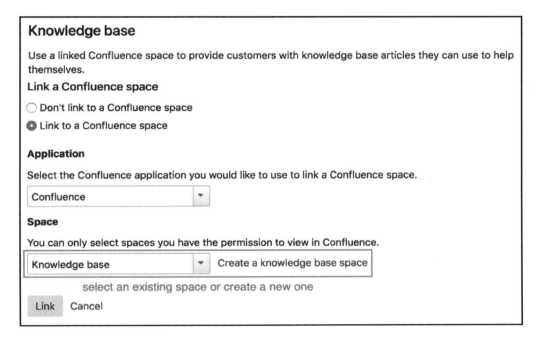

4. Click on the **Link** button after you have selected or created your knowledge base Confluence space.

The last step is to configure the knowledge base access controls so that autosearching the portal will return results. If both Jira Service Desk and Confluence are connected to the same user repository, such as an LDAP, then they should have the same user accounts. Make sure you grant end users read access to the knowledge base space and give page access to your agents.

Once you have set up a knowledge base, there will be a new section called **Related knowledge base articles** for the agent's view. An agent can create a new knowledge base article by performing the following steps:

1. Click on the **create an article** link:

2. Enter the title for the new article, select a label, and then select the template to use for the article's content.

3. Click on the **Create** button. This will take you to the article in Confluence, which will be prepopulated, based on the selected template. You can edit the content and publish it when ready:

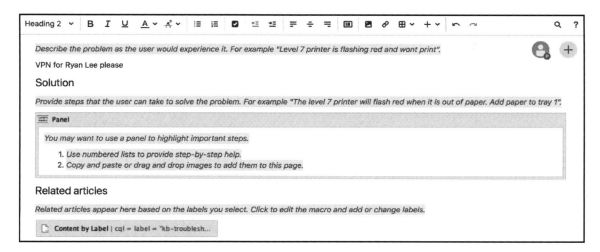

It's now time to see how these steps work.

How it works...

By integrating Jira and Confluence through an application link, we created a one-to-one mapping of a Jira service desk and Confluence space. Whenever an agent clicks on the **create an article** link from a request, they will create a new page in the mapped Confluence space, based on the selected template.

Confluence comes with two default templates to use for the knowledge base: **how to** and **troubleshooting**. You can add more templates to Confluence, and they will be available for your agents when they want to create new articles.

By setting up a knowledge base for your service desk, search results will include knowledge base articles when your customers perform a search from your portal. This is shown in the following screenshot as well:

Jira Service Desk will also automatically suggest articles based on the customer's input when raising new requests, helping them to get solutions more quickly, and avoiding the duplication of requests and your team's efforts.

Collaborating with your internal teams on service requests

The traditional workflow of a service desk involves a customer raising a request, and an agent working with the customer to come up with a solution. This usually works in scenarios where the problem is simple and straightforward to solve. However, in many real-world situations, the problem can be complicated and may require multiple people from different teams to collaborate together in order to resolve it.

In this recipe, we will explore how to collaborate with people outside of the standard support team. Normally, you will run a single Jira instance host for both your service desk and engineering projects, so it is very easy to collaborate together in a single system. In this recipe, we will look at a more complex scenario, where the support team is using a Jira Service Desk instance, and the engineering team is using a separate Jira Software instance, and both teams are working together on resolving a customer's request.

How to do it...

The first step is to create an application link between your Jira Service Desk instance and the Jira Software instance. You can refer to the *Integrating Jira with other Jira instances* recipe in `Chapter 7`, *Integrations with Jira*, for detailed information. If you have already integrated both Jira instances, you can skip these steps:

1. Navigate to **Administration** > **Applications** > **Application links**.
2. Enter the Jira Software instance's URL, and create the application link. Jira should automatically detect the target application as Jira. If, for some reason, it does not do so, then make sure you select Jira as the **Application** type when prompted:

Once you have linked both Jira instances, the agent and/or collaborator will be able to link the request in your service desk to the issue in the engineering project:

1. Browse to the request in the service desk.
2. Select the **Link** option under the **More** menu.
3. Select the Jira Software instance from the **Server** drop-down list.
4. Choose the relationship between the request and issue. Usually, you should use the **is caused by** option.
5. Select the issue to link to the request. You can type in the issue key directly if you know it; otherwise, you can click on the **search for an issue** link to run a search.

6. Make sure the **Create reciprocal link** option is checked so that a link will also be created for the issue. This will let the engineers know that there is a customer request pending on the resolution of the issue, and will help the engineering team to prioritize their tasks.

7. Select the **Internal comment** tab if you want to add a comment to provide additional details to the agent working on the request. Comments added in this way will not be visible to the customer.

8. Click on the **Link** button to create the link.

The screen looks like the following screenshot:

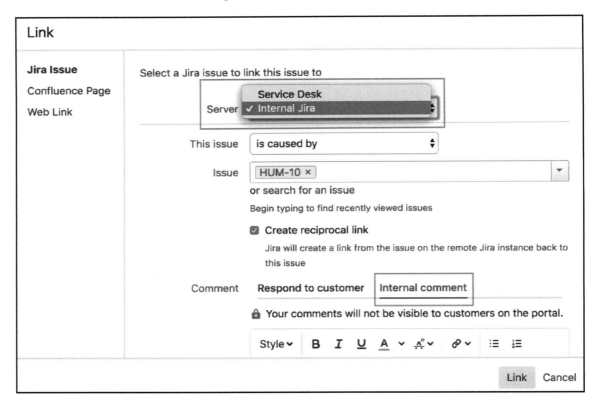

Now let's take a look at how these steps work.

How it works...

The Jira platform has an out-of-the-box feature called an application link, which allows you to integrate multiple instances of Atlassian products together—in this case, Jira Service Desk and Jira Software. By creating an application link between the two, our Jira Service Desk is able to recognize our Jira Software instance and access the data it has and, specifically, any issues.

Once we have created an issue link between the customer request and the engineering issue, both systems will be able to query and display each other's status. This means that when an agent looks at the request, they will also be able to see the status of the linked engineering issue, even if it is from a different system. Look at the following screenshot:

Once the engineer completes the issue, the agent will see the status update automatically from within the request.

Tracking and evaluating performance with an SLA

An SLA helps you to measure the level of service performance of your team, and also provides insights into where improvements can be made.

In this recipe, we will set up a new SLA metric for our service desk, where we will measure the amount of time it takes for the team to solve customer requests. However, we will not take into account the amount of time spent waiting for additional information from customers.

How to do it...

To set up the SLAs, perform the following steps:

1. Browse to the service desk that you want to set up SLAs for.
2. Click on the **Project settings** option in the lower-left corner of the screen.
3. Select the **SLAs** option from the panel on the left-hand side.
4. Click on the **Create SLA** option.
5. Enter a new name for the new SLA:

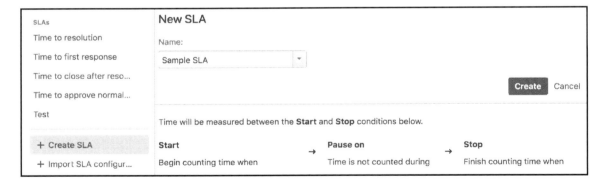

Before you can create the new SLA metric by clicking on the **Create** button, you will first need to define how time will be measured:

1. Select the **Issue Created** option from the **Start** column.
2. Select the **Status: Waiting for customer** option from the **Pause on** column.
3. Select the **Entered Status: Resolved** option from the **Stop** column:

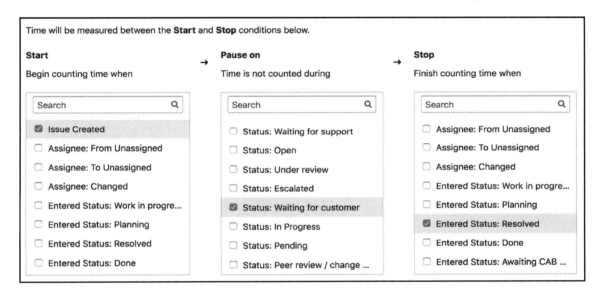

After we have configured our time-counting rules, we need to set our SLA goals so that we can measure the team's performance:

1. Enter `priority = High` in the **Issues (JQL)** text field.
2. Set the **Goal** to `12h`, which is 12 hours.
3. Select **Default 24/7 calendar** if you want the SLA to be calculated to include non-working hours; otherwise, select **Sample 9-5 Calendar** if you only want to include working hours. Then, click on the **Add** button.

You can repeat the three preceding steps to add more goals, and, once you are ready, click on the **Create** button to create the new SLA metric:

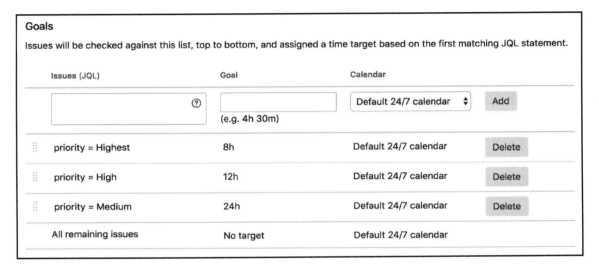

This completes the steps for this recipe. Let's take a look at how these steps actually work.

How it works...

Jira Service Desk's SLAs are composed of two parts: how time is to be calculated and the goal to achieve under the given criteria. The goal setting part is quite straightforward:

- **A JQL query to define the rule**: For example, `priority = High` means that all requests within the project with their priority set to **High** will have this SLA goal.
- **The goal to achieve specified in time**: For example, **8h** means the goal for this SLA is 8 hours.
- **The calendar to use**: This defines the time and day when calculating whether the SLA goal has been met.

The actual SLA calculation part is slightly more complex. When calculating SLA, we need to define the following:

- **When to start counting**: This is defined in the **Start** column. In our recipe, we selected the **Issue Created** option, which means that the SLA will start counting as soon as a customer has created a request.
- **When to stop counting**: This is defined in the **Stop** column. In our recipe, we selected the **Entered Status: Resolved** option, which means that as soon as an agent puts the request into the **Resolved** workflow status, the SLA will stop counting.
- **When to pause counting**: This is optional, and is defined in the **Pause on** column. In our recipe, we selected the **Status: Waiting for customer** option; this means that once an agent has requested additional information from the customer, the SLA will be paused. Once the customer has provided the requested information, the SLA will resume counting again.

Other Books You May Enjoy

If you enjoyed this book, you may be interested in these other books by Packt:

Jira 8 Essentials - Fifth Edition
Patrick Li

ISBN: 9781789802818

- Understand Jira's data hierarchy and how to design and work with projects in Jira
- Use Jira for agile software projects, business process management, customer service support, and more
- Understand issues and work with them
- Design both system and custom fields to behave differently under different contexts
- Create and design your own screens and apply them to different project and issue types
- Gain an understanding of the workflow and its various components
- Set up both incoming and outgoing mail servers to work with e-mails

Jira Quick Start Guide
Ravi Sagar

ISBN: 9781789342673

- Implement Jira as a project administrator or project manager
- Get familiar with various functionalities of Jira
- Configure projects and boards in your organisation's Jira instance
- Understand how and when to use components and versions in your projects
- Manage project configurations and Jira schemes
- Learn the best practices to manage your Jira instance

Leave a review - let other readers know what you think

Please share your thoughts on this book with others by leaving a review on the site that you bought it from. If you purchased the book from Amazon, please leave us an honest review on this book's Amazon page. This is vital so that other potential readers can see and use your unbiased opinion to make purchasing decisions, we can understand what our customers think about our products, and our authors can see your feedback on the title that they have worked with Packt to create. It will only take a few minutes of your time, but is valuable to other potential customers, our authors, and Packt. Thank you!

Index

P

password policies
  setting up 142, 143, 144, 145
permissions
  troubleshooting 212
project role memberships
  managing 107, 108
project roles
  managing 104, 105, 106
project-specific email address
  setting up 177
project
  access, controlling to 129, 130, 131
  customized screens, setting up for 47, 48, 49, 50
  issue types, setting up 40, 41
  workflows, setting up for 68, 69, 70, 71
provider 194
public user signup
  enabling 100, 101, 102

R

remember me cookies
  duration, modifying of 149
report 238
Resolve transitions 73

S

Salesforce
  reference 204
ScriptRunner
  reference 226
scripts
  executing, in Jira 226, 227, 228
Seraph framework
  reference 150
service desk portal
  customizing 236, 237, 238
service principal name (SPN) 120
service requests
  information, capturing from customers for 239, 242, 243
  internal teams, collaborating on 248, 249, 251
services 222

shared filters
  managing 233, 234
Simple Mail Transfer Protocol (SMTP) 154
single sign-on (SSO) 115
single sign-on functionality
  setting up, with Crowd 116
  setting up, with crowd 115, 117
single sign-on
  setting up, with Google 117, 119
SLA
  calculating 255
  used, for evaluating performance 252, 254
  used, for tracking performance 252, 254
Slack
  Jira, integrating with 195, 196, 197, 198, 199
SSL certificates
  installing, from applications 27, 28
SSL
  setting up 21, 23, 25, 26
statuses 68
Summary field 43
switch user (SU) 229

T

Team 52
transitions 68
trigger types
  integrations 225
  issue triggers 225
  scheduled 225

U

Universal Plugin Manager (UPM) 217
  reference 57, 77
user input
  validating, in workflow transition 80, 81
user sessions
  switching, in Jira 229, 230
user
  allowing, to control permissions 134, 135, 136, 137, 138
  deactivating 108
  importing, from LDAP 109, 111, 112
  integrating, from LDAP 109, 111, 112

W

webhook 179
Windows domain single sign-on
  setting up 119, 120, 123
workflow transition bar
  rearranging 86, 87, 88
workflow transition logic
  creating 92, 93, 94, 95, 96

workflow transition
  additional processing, performance 82, 83, 84
  availability, restricting 77, 78, 79
  field required, creating 90, 91, 92
  information, capturing 72
  resolution values, restricting 88, 89
  user input, validating in 80, 81
workflow
  setting up, for project 68, 69, 70, 71

Made in the USA
Coppell, TX
04 November 2021